THE FLOCK THAT
BRAVED ME

NATALIE JEAN

WESTBOW
PRESS®
A DIVISION OF THOMAS NELSON
& ZONDERVAN

WestBow Press books may be ordered through booksellers or by contacting:

WestBow Press
A Division of Thomas Nelson & Zondervan
1663 Liberty Drive
Bloomington, IN 47403
www.westbowpress.com
844-714-3454

Scripture quotations are taken from the Holy Bible, New Living Translation, copyright © 1996, 2004, 2015 by Tyndale House Foundation. Used by permission of Tyndale House Publishers Inc., Carol Stream, Illinois 60188. All rights reserved.

ISBN: 979-8-3850-3852-7 (sc)
ISBN: 979-8-3850-3851-0 (e)

Library of Congress Control Number: 2024924904

Print information available on the last page.

WestBow Press rev. date: 11/27/2024

Jailed free

· ·

It is a Saturday morning, the morning I woke up released from my ankle monitor they served my favorite breakfast at 2:45 AM. Eggs and oatmeal with applesauce, since the removal of my chain or shackles if you will I've smiled differently and had a whole new perception of free. I am free from my sin, I am forgiven, Jesus has completely transformed my soul, my spirit, my outlook, trust and my heart. After I basically licked the applesauce from my tray I put my makeshift sleeves from the socks back on my tiny cold arms and stuck my ear plugs made from the gloves they wear when the trustees serve our trays, you cut the finger holes off stuff them with just the right amount of toilet paper and tie them, shove them in your ears so you can muffle the constant toilet flushes and 50 plus voices that surround you 24/7. I curled back up into my fetal like position on bunk 18 with a full belly, smiled and said to God thank you so much for my favorite meal. It's still pretty dim lighted in here as I woke up abruptly with an intense feeling of wholeness. I started crying under my blanket thanking God again for being my father! I finally feel and I mean I felt his hug, his presence, his peace and comfort. I feel safe. I was having a dream well several weird ones at first but the one that woke me up I was walking into a huge garage like building, mechanic shop type situation. We were talking about my car before bed, but that's another story. I walked in actually I was like skipping like a child. I had just spoke to the front shop mechanics there were two men, handsome one resembled the gentleman who removed my ankle monitor, very tall, light pale skinned and soft orange hair. They couldn't tell me where to find the parts I needed so I skipped to the back where I couldn't see the mechanic but it was my dad, God saying I've got you. Don't worry, let me fix these parts then you can drive it again. I had one very flat tire and one kind of low on air tire. Then the lights turned on in the mechanic shop and I woke up with the best tears rolling down my face. That's when I knew I am OK. I am safe, God is my father and I finally feel it y'all! I kept reciting in my head don't you worry my father walks on water. Good Lord I feel better than yesterday y'all. Only thing now I think these eggs and oatmeal I love so much are about to be released too! Which toilet number should I go to? We have got six options and some beautifully rolled toilet paper by one of the girls here called big Bertha, she's one of my favorite flock ladies. I guess since I have so much time to dabble into my thoughts I could share on how I got to my flock. I call it my flock because the TV shows and what not I watch before I was assigned here call it a pod or alpha eight, A8 bunk 18. I was reading scripture before bed, rack up one night and my brother ole Luke 12:32 do not be afraid, little flock for your father has chosen gladly to give you the Kingdom. Grazed upon my puffy tear cried eyes. Every night since then I pictured my father God placing his widespread arms like a blanket over each bunk filled with anxious hearts and scooping us up for a good night's rest. Now if you want to know I chose potty #5. I'm usually the first one up laying on my bunk wondering when I can come out of my bed but not really because it's ice cold in here and wearing socks on your arms is not allowed.

Bunny trails And coffee rails

TODAY IS EASTER. I SIGNED UP FOR RECREATION AT 8:30 AM SO HOPEFULLY I can go hop off some of this energy from my hummingbird heart. I miss Madi more than ever today. I don't think I've ever spent a holiday without her since she was born. Oh man, I can't think like that because now the tears are accumulating in the back of my throat. I ended up being able to get my work out on and my body up to my heart rate during rec earlier, which in all honesty felt fantastic. Then I cried myself to a nap after thinking about Madi and her as a wild toddler around this time every year up until now when I can't hug or see her. I've had a lot of epiphany moments but I was talking to which we call her the Michelin girl her words not mine, about our pictures on our little flock ID's and she looks like a wild mess because she was on a crystal meth spree apparently and hadn't slept or ate in over a week. I told her what in the world would be fun about that, she was cute and just laughed like it wasn't killing her inside, but I knew it was, and I said a little prayer in my head for her and myself at this moment. Yall, I just want to let you know that my doctor prescribed me a medication that was basically legalized meth and it kind of infuriates me, because I see the effects stuff like this has on people and the control it takes of their lives. Doctors and pharmacists do not care it is a money driven business, but I pray that God shows her and continues to show me a different way of life. Me conversing with the Michelin girl was just complete clarity and a seal of approval that my God no longer wants substances to be part of my life. Honestly ladies, as much as I hate to say this, I coincidentally love this place and I'm not just writing that. I have had a lot of much needed cleansing time to be out of the world I was in to show me what it's not supposed to be like. I need God my father the minimum amount of food and rest and no substance or person to fulfill what God has already planned for me. This goes for you too ladies. We must believe this, my mom always said you can wish in one hand and you know what in the other one and see which one fills up faster, the you know what! I finally and truly believe in the words I've been reading in scripture and what I've been trying to understand and feel for 39 years. Philippians 4:6-13 Do not be anxious about anything but in everything by prayer and supplication with Thanksgiving let your request be made known to God and the peace of God which surpasses all understanding will guard your hearts and your minds in Christ Jesus. Finally, brothers, whatever is honorable, whatever is just, whatever is pure, whatever is lovely, whatever is commendable if there is any excellence. If there is anything worthy of praise think about these things. I have learned in whatever situation I am how to be content. All these words I've skimmed through for so long or tried getting my streaks on the Bible app now they all make sense. Girls can we get an Amen! I yearn to learn more and more about what I'm reading and understand the why, how and who. I'm not a bible thumper but I have fallen so deeply in love with my father my God my Jesus, it's moved me to a place of peace. That's why I say the flock that braved me. How I got here why I am here and no I am not gay for this stay but I'll scripture my way through this stay. These words were here all along but in order for me to feel the hugs and love for my father God, Jesus who died on the cross for my, our sins, God knew I had to be broken to the complete core and go through all the bull you know what I wished for knowing that hand was filling up with bull honkey. I love this presence in this flock, I pray for all of us I pray for you the reader although a real Human hug would be nice, and I will never take those for granted again. Hugs are my new drugs. Can I get an RX for those ladies. I'm telling you this horse dookie I wished for in a man filled up my cup and didn't allow room for what God had already planned for not only me but my best friend, my heart my first true love Madison Jean. All this time all the red flags were ignored, and I didn't allow God's grace or path through so he locked me up, two-fold On God like Madi would say.

April fools

4/2/24 WELL, I GOT APRIL FOOLED BUT I BUILT THAT UP IN MY OWN HEAD because I figured my father, who walks on water would make my exit from this place humorous. But my time and assignment are not done which is fine I'm trying hard not to place the blame on anyone or anything but myself and what I'm meant to serve for during this mini devilcation at this pre flock. I guess my assignment is to uplift and speak what I know to each individual little flock nugget that comes across my path. There is another flock mate with the name Natalie, and I've been praying with her that she be set free because she's done her time little did, we know it prayers work because she was called to leave today. You would think if I could pray other people out of here, I could pray my way out of here. Even though I have cried myself to sleep probably every night since I got to my bunk, I don't feel too sad during the day. Last night there was a country song on you've got a fast car which made me think of Madi because she always plays this on her country playlist, oh come on Madi if you have a fast car come and rescue your Mama.

Now that I've had all these grand epiphanies, I feel free to be honest. Free of my sin, free of judgment, free of my ankle monitor that cursed me and labeled me. I am a child of God I have eternal life and not one judge, lawyer, cop, Sergeant or human on this earth will ever have power over my thoughts and my confidence or who I am again. My father has put the deepest desire in yearning for me to trust the process of what, who and why. Be a positive, encouraging, uplifting little light to those who cross my path. I can with all my heart say I will never drink alcohol again or abuse prescriptions just because of a irresponsible doctor that gave them to me. I didn't need that all I needed was my father's acknowledgement and I got it twofold. Put the ankle monitor on me then locked me up and I know those two things were the best things to ever happen to me!

They can't kill my soul
or crush my spirit

EVEN THOUGH I KEEP READING GOOD SCRIPTURES AND I'M FAITHFUL that the Lord's word is above all other these flesh suits walking around or should I now call them sparrows keep chirping horrible news, news of you won't see a counselor for a long time to the number amount of days we have left in each color shirt to taking outside rec because of a little rain. Then a monitor who I prayed for after she told me for the third time, y'all I sit crisscross applesauce on my box and she told me to put my feet down. I felt the sudden urge to pray for her because I feel she has some insecurities and demons because y'all I'm tiny as a bug I can be on my box little as I need but I just said yes ma'am and put my legs down. Y'all the rules are so uncalled for how about you let me talk to my counselor or probation officer or someone other than eating and showering and watching flocking TV but again I'll say that the Lord has placed it on my heart not only to pray for the sparrows in my flock, y'all I can't even believe I read that word again what the flock, but to create this testimony for you, yes you, you beautiful person reading these words as I write them live and in action on April 16th at 10:50 AM as I sit on my box little blue box feet on the blessed ground and wait to walk to chow yet again. I'm trying so hard not to get written up but the littlest things set these sparrows off in my flock. Wow, I love how this is all coming together who would have thunk it yes I know that's bad English but who would have thunk it Natalie Chapman bunk 18 in my first flock bunk one in my final flock would be given the weapons and specialized armor and equipment to not only be in the present and learn, listen and understand but write this testimony that as Jesus said is how I will yell it on house tops all while my heart hugs and my father is grabbing my hand the whole time. Y'all just wow I want to physically hug you the reader right now but I am definitely in the middle of nowhere and no contact is in place but I'll send you a heart hug now, you are loved you are strong, you are not alone even if it feels that way in the flesh, listen and look around close your eyes and pray and God will send you that heart hug you need. I shall go walk the catwalk and I just thought of my kitties at home ohh how I missed them can't talk about them because I don't want to cry on my way to chow, bone appetite. It's 11:55 now and as I get back from chow and we sit on our boxes while some ladies decide to take up time to go potty and put their long sleeves on under their colored shirt I will share the heart hugs I got. Firstly the rain came down hard earlier because the ground was wet and it felt sticky and muggy as we walked the catwalk. I heard birds chirping and asked God to heart hug me then in the middle of a pretty large area there were two white tiny little flowers basically staring at me in my eyes. They stood out so distinct I laughed and smiled and probably seemed absurd to whomever saw me but I didn't care. Then a tune popped into my head not only the rescue song but I said Jesus if I focus on you I'll make it through, if I focus on you I'll make it through. A part in Matthew right before we left for chow was to not love anyone other than God focus on him. So I will and I do, I trust you Lord I also laughed at myself to myself because I said in my head to my father I can talk to you all day long and never get in trouble cute right? I do talk to him all day then I write what he puts on my heart the Holy Spirit moves my pen I swear, constant heart hugs and little reminders that he is with me. I love my Lord and my father so much it brings me to happy tears when I think about how far I've gotten because of him and him alone. I just remember laying in the bunk in my pre flock crying under the blanket, then when I was almost too tired and scared to get through that place anymore and he sent me the man telling me I was leaving that place. God worked his amazing magic and got me out of there in 23 days. Every time I tell flesh suits that I was only there for 23 days they are amazed, and you know what I say every single time, I prayed my way out and Jesus pulled me out of there! Seriously that was only my first mini miracle which all led me to reading the book of Matthew because if y'all remember I said I started with the book of John, Philippians, Romans then the New Testament in the book of Matthew. I never got my blue Bible in the first flock because the Holy Spirit knew I need the Bible they will give me here. I'm actually borrowing one from the little library here so I can't make my heart hugs notes in it but I requested one the first day I got here. So I should get one soon. Seriously though because if I brought that Bible from jail they would have locked it away anyway with the little private property I came with when I came here with nothing and this book I am writing isn't that amazing? The sparrow flesh suit that did my intake thank the Lord, let me bring my notebook pages because I think I may have caused a scene otherwise. God knew exactly what I needed and it was my paper and pen clothed with armor God I flocking love you and seriously can't wait for the first person to read this book and tell me what they think. I know the beginning when I'm in flock 1 is a little more humorous but it did not always feel that way y'all I just want to try to encourage and power and to put a smile on that beautiful face smile now as you read this because there is a heart hug that you may have needed I closed my eyes and pictured where this book would end up and in whose hands, yours. I know God loves you and if you believe that to be true you are forgiven loved and have eternal life these are not my words they are right there in that Bible you probably have next to your bed, on a dusty bookshelf or maybe on your bunk temporary house of the at the foot of your bunk with your toiletry items and commissary bag covered by your only hand towel. Maybe it's in your box by your bunk in front of it open that Bible right now and you did dig deeper than you ever had before and I promise you that life will start amazing you keep this testimony close to your heart too if you want or share it with someone you love who needs hope. Y'all we have to be here for one another even when we are locked up, incarcerated in a rehab place or even alone at home in our beds. There is only one thing getting me through this and that is the love of my father and his son Jesus who died on the cross for my sins and yours the Holy Spirit y'all it's flocking real and it's in me. I wouldn't just say that I flocking believe it and you should too by this far along in my testimony keep reading ladies because the big finale is yet to come I can feel it getting closer and closer every day I am knocking banging on the door I am digging deep into my Bible and all around me looking for signs and heart hugs. I am asking every other minute of every day to be rescued from this place and storm then I am also waiting and listening to the Holy Spirit. I have to trust his timing and plans are not mine I only fear my Lord y'all and it's not scary because I trust and love him so much I'm not afraid anymore. There is not one sparrow or flesh suit that can kill my spirit. God's been with me this whole time. Stay focused on God and you'll get through whatever it is you're facing let's face it together read these words as they jump start to your own testimony get a pen out and you start writing down all the heart hugs and even bad things that flesh suits say and do, take note of your life ladies. Put that substance or addiction down for just a sober minute and pray with me, God I know the plans you have for me are those of good, addiction free, sober minded and for love and trust and eternal life. I trust you Lord my father in his name I, we pray Amen. Now wipe your tears away, I had to as well and let's do this we are better together. I love you and I don't know you yet but maybe I will, if not we can continue to be spirit sisters. I got your back girl I'm praying for you right now. I just took some inventory of how much I've written in this testimony and from the pages I have numbered, landings me at 58 pages. I didn't think I had that much to say but I guess when you can't talk out loud, letting it all out on paper, well here we are holy testimony. I am going to cherish this thing when I am done completing it. Now I'm over here wondering what other books I can write then I had a funny not so funny thing crossed my little brain epiphany if you will. In my sobriety and recovery outside of here I was in school to become an LCDC y'all know that but if you skipped that page well now you know. I've always wanted to help encourage and empower women. My daughter and I tried starting a podcast and we didn't know how to start or what to talk about. Y'all I wanted it so bad. I watched people like Mel Robbins, Rachel Hollis always love me some Oprah W. and was attending online school. God flipping knew I didn't learn that way, remember I am a hands-on learner, I must see, touch and feel. So thank you for prayers answered, not how I saw them play out by any means, but honestly, the best most amazing way possible answered he abundantly answered them because I am getting the whole shebang raw live no blooper takeouts and I'm recording my life day for day through the grace of God because my testimony of how he got me through what I want to teach and be a coach for in life free from addiction of any kind and live in full 1000% Infinity trust and belief that my God, your God, our God is real. Through heart hugs and again heart hugs are signs from the Holy Spirit. The spirit is in me and I am being guided by that truth love and his way. This book should give you goosebumps, spirit bumps. Bam a chapter of the book name a heart hug. See that's the Holy Spirit y'all God is literally using my need and want and faith and love for him to be obedient to what he has called me to do. Then when you're reading this you too will experience these things because it will have the stamp of approval from my father. I'm being led to feircefully prepare this for you. Nothing happens by mistake each heart hug happened exactly the way God intended it to. I just wrote it as I was moved to that's how I know for certain the big finale of my testimony will be the full of fireworks like are you flocking kidding me, did that just really happen kind of moment. I know it in my heart to be true. A testimony of his love for me, you and us will only be of that to show you the reader how if you stay obedient to God and trust in him and only him your life will be saved. He will come and rescue you no matter where you are. It is not absurd, it's not luck it's my father God and Jesus and the Holy Spirit y'all it's incredible. I had to pause and take a little crying moment because I felt that so much in my heart writing it that I reread it and it touched me even more. God I thank you for my life and the love you have shown me that you have forgiven me and that you too forgive and love all who chose you trust you and believe in you I pray for whoever is reading this and myself as I write this to feel those heart hugs in the chaos, in the noise when the flesh suits are yapping in our ears that we only hear you and your words your truth. That those who seek find you, those who knock you open the door and call them by name, those who ask receive in your name Jesus Christ, Amen! Sorry ladies I just felt a holy moment it was and is in me I just can't stop I love you ladies I love holy moments they feel good right. I'm going to take a handbrake and read some Matthew for my soul. I have a blister from writing so much y'all spirit blister bump. Y'all I'm reading the parable of a farmer scattering seed and going to try to understand it and break it down how the Lord puts it on my heart. This is a good one; blessed are your eyes because they see and your ears because they hear. Seeds were spread along and hit a footpath made of soil add some pebbles and rocks soil pebbles and rocks represent us the flesh who were meant to either retain them soak them in and regrow them but before that happened sparrows or birds and fleshed souls came and ate the seeds plucking away what God put out for us some flesh lost altogether some were on the rocky part of the footpath and some didn't sink in to say but those with a good foundation were the seeds sunk in, into the soil grew new life and spread. So think of that as building your life in a good soil so when your seed is planted in your heart it will flourish and grow. God can only plant a good seed in your life if your bones are good. I know y'all understand that, if the bones are good nothing else matters it spoke to me to ensure that when you start your journey or if you're already deep in the journey our foundation is always important so we can stay true to the Lord. Now I have that song in my head and I keep picturing a skeleton with weak brittle bones crumbling. I have always looked at my wrist and ankles and shins and wondered what my skeleton looks like that was random but I thought y'all would enjoy that. I think it's almost time to go to chow y'all Yee Haw guess the Holy Spirit is lifting mine today to lift yours. Life is too short not to laugh, so find a moment in the chaos, in jail and rehab in or under the bridge and laugh at yourself. Laugh with others love is what makes the world go round and without love and laughter our spirits will dwindle away

White butterflies

···

FOCUS ON YOU LORD YOU WILL GET ME THROUGH. I SAID IT MANY TIMES on my way to chow, during and on the way back y'all. I didn't know there were white butterflies. I've seen black and all other colors but don't recall white ones, heart hugs. I looked all around for them then a big black one grazed my pathway on the way back. I smiled as I spoke to my father the whole time we are definitely besties I continually say I trust you and I love you over and over in my thoughts. It's wild how much peace he brings you when you need it and even when you don't know you need it so thank you again to my love my rock the Lord. Every one is now getting ready to watch TV again I'm of course writing to y'all my spirit sisters I just brushed my teeth too after chow because y'all I love apples but I feel like they get caught in my tooth that gives me problems and y'all I can't be having tooth pain in here that would not be good so the good Lord prompted me right when I got to the bathroom to brush my choppers. I miss taking my vitamins and using peroxide on my teeth as mouthwash. I've been using the smallest toothbrush possible for over a month now both flocks have the same gadgets for us. I guess Tuesdays go by slow because we don't meet with a counselor and I still haven't talked to anyone who was supposed to set up my plan or whatever. At this point I'm not even worried because I know my God is the one who knows the truth about me, Natalie and he calls me by name and he hasn't forgot about me. I'm focused on what plans he has for me because the sparrows as were mentioned earlier have no say or will over my life. I know this to be true I'm getting heart hugs all around to just stay obedient to God and follow the lead with the Holy Spirit so I'm going to read the part in Matthew when Jesus walks on water because I said that a lot in my pre flock. I believe it to be true; Matthew 14:27 but Jesus spoke to them at once don't be afraid he said take courage I am here at about 3:00am in the morning Jesus came toward them walking on water, they were terrified. I'm not sure why in the mother of Mary they would be scared because I take this as something amazing and wonderful and I have such a creative mind I can picture this especially because I always used to wake up around 3:00 AM and it kind of makes sense I needed to pray in the dark like I did in my first flock. I do here well I pray way more than that at night here I'm in constant communication with my father even writing this I feel like I'm talking to not only you the reader but my father. I love it y'all I'm telling you if you're ever in a place where you aren't allowed to speak out loud pray to God your father read his word and write your conversation with him it is the best form of therapy. Hello heart hug I don't need one of those counselors to judge me or even listen to or hear me because my father already has and does wow another heart hug comfort. I just released the want to meet a counselor in here because mine's been at work this whole time God. Thank you for your unfailing never ending no judgment love thank you for healing my heart from the sin that bound me to poor choices wow I love you Lord and I trust you. Seriously he has been here all along Lord knows I don't need any more flesh suits or sparrows stoning me judging me, falsely accusing me. What a great epiphany no more grievances to speak with a person who ultimately doesn't care about my heart and soul the way that my father does. In Romans there are so many verses and scriptures I wrote down that declare this so again Forget you Satan and all your devil puppets if the Lord is for me who can be against me. No one that matters, the love I feel right now by my Lord my savior and father is unexplainable. By writing this testimony my needs I think I need from flesh keep getting awakened by the Lords grace because he's already taken over the pen y'all. I gave him my heart, my soul and my life. I love him far beyond any other love I can know. I feel at peace right now and comfort waiting patiently for my rescue. I will document all these learnings and heart hugs from scripture. I feel so lucky to feel this way given my circumstances. If y'all physically saw me you would think everything, but I'm sitting on a hard blue treasure chest away from home hairy, but clean, tired from the flesh suits but in love and content that my father is here with me the Holy Spirit is and has been phenomenally wonderful to me and through me. I hope and pray you too feel these feelings of joy peace and love I'm going to pray my way out of here and through here. I really want to find that story about when Jesus said roll up your bed in the middle of the night but I can't quite find it, but the whole part of Romans is fantastic y'all. I can't copy all of it but I do know that it says for where your treasure is so there your heart will be not that this blue treasure box thing is my personal treasure chest but it holds this Bible and my book to you the reader with my deepest heart testimony so that's a kind of heart hug. My back is really starting to hurt today y'all I can't wait to be rescued and actually sleep in a bed that has a mattress and pillows I'm getting too old for a floor like my top bunk but I am grateful I have a safe place to lay my head at night and I know my father is for sure not going to let me his daughter suffer too much longer. I kind of feel like the sparrows and flesh mates are catching wind of my spirit they can control my physical movements and say things to try and crush me, but my father will save me from this flock. They won't be able to stop it or persecute me any longer y'all. I watched the part of the movie that is on called "The Son of God" which is Jesus dying on the cross and there's a rainbow in the scene after he dies on the cross he asks for water then a slight rainbow is in the circle around the cross, heart hug rainbow style. That brought my love for rainbows back to surface then I started crying when the song Mary did you know came on, when it says he walked on water y'all I love the Lord the son Jesus and the Holy Spirit thank you Lord for showing me all this before bedtime. I needed sweet dreams. Ladies take some deep time tonight before you lay your head down and pray the devil out of your situation. He's listening, he loves you and me all these things I've been writing about and praying and the words, epiphanies are directly from the Holy Spirit. I literally sit back close my eyes and meditate on the word of God and then am a heart hugged. Remember too ladies, I know you may be in a place where you may clearly not want to be or maybe you know deep down your right where you need to be or maybe you have judges, lawyers, parents, boyfriends, sisters, brothers or grandparents or any flesh suit falsely accuse or misrepresent you. I wrote about that in previous chapters let them. Be locked up, for the words you'll use if you believe in God your father will come from the Holy Spirit. Trust that he will guide you through the storm, there will still be rain, pain, sorrow and loneliness. Lightning and thunder but if you take his hand and allow him to fill up your heart, your cup you will get through whatever he puts in front of you. Look how far I've come. I don't know your journey or where you are in your walk with God but even if you start today ladies, he already knows you, every strand of your hair he knows your name he has already planned for your life. Listen, follow and love but most importantly don't stop believing even when the judges, the lawyers, flesh suits, sparrows or devil puppets try to haunt, deceive and condemn you pray for them, love them and grab his hand. Hold that Bible, dig into it, reread what you don't understand and ask God to dummy it up. He does it for me, he knows how you learn he knew you before you were created. He is the truth the way and the life, plus ladies take a look at what you're going through whether good or bad at this moment and if you think it could help someone, yall it share it. The good the bad and the ugly, you are not ugly you are beautiful, brave and strong that's why you picked up this book, because maybe a flock saved you too. Maybe you'll save a flock, maybe we can help save sparrows who knows. Yep I did that on purpose, but seriously you may be just the story someone needs to hear for recovery, abuse, addiction, judgment or just be a light in someone's darkness. I want to add a little glitter to your darkness, sparkle to the rain, rainbow to your storm. I hope you sleep well tonight or if you're reading this in the morning I hope you enjoy your coffee, have a wonderful day or if you're well, wherever you are whatever you're doing do it in the glory of your father who gracefully walks on water. Side note ladies, when I talk about this testimony I tell everyone the Holy Spirit is in me and God is real and alive in me. I love talking about Jesus and my father, and you should too.

Changes

Now I know why in my pre-flock I always woke up at like 4:00 or 5:00 AM because it was preparing me for my final flock. I also wrote about how in the pre flock the early bird does not get the worm but here you can pee or go #2 in peace and pre brush your teeth that way when everyone else wakes up you just have to go change your shirt really quick. Y'all I'm a military brat. I'm aware of the structure and rules but I also believe they should be enforced properly and not meant to single anyone out like they unfortunately do here. It has already happened to me. What's bizarre is I observe everything, and I overheard a guard say they have been here for 10 years. I'm thinking, you've been here that long, and you haven't improved things. It's the sparrow I had to pray for because I can see broken and hurt deep inside her. There are only two sparrows I've met so far that I can see take care of their body and have awesome spirits. I won't name names but it's sad that someone would remain in a position as this and still be bitter and demeaning after 10 years. Don't worry though y'all no one can kill my spirit or soul. We read about that in the book Matthew yesterday. So, there are three greens up front and center at 5:15 AM reciting things from books. One is a recovery book, but they are just reading the words robotic style. Then the tired flock mates clap robotically. This is by no means uplifting. What uplifts me is the excitement I get from waking up to grab my Bible and these words, this testimony is what's keeping me alive. Y'all we aren't here for drama and friendships they need to dig into their bibles all the girls just keep talking about not breaking the rules so we can get home why don't we focus on falling in love with God so we can be rescued. I fear this place is broken. I'm so happy yesterday happened though and I had all the epiphanies I had about my counselor being Jesus the Holy Spirit. I don't need the flesh suits trying to explain this flock life. This life is nothing like real life. On the way to chow we walked by the intake room where your journey begins here, we were stopped along the way and with my good flipping ears I heard their conversation as the guard was talking to them, and all I could hear is those blessed numbered days that you're stuck here. That's all the sparrows put in your mind and heart when you arrive and that's such a scary thing. I'm praying for those ladies to have the strength to focus on what's important in here regardless of the lack of actual communication and help. I pray they come across this book. I pray they get a Bible right away get locked into the Lord, let's get locked into the Lord not locked up. No Sparrow, no flock mate, no flesh suit has say over the number of days I'm here, only the Lord my father does. Same for you.

On one of the first days here I remember a sparrow, a flesh suit talking to us about the other sparrows who would be working for the next few days, and she said that this is a game. The days are numbered, and our status is colored because they want to see who's new and who's close to leaving, y'all this is far beyond not oK. I've witnessed it first-hand too even though I'm up and out of my bed first since I'm in red, I am last to change, shower or go to the restroom even though some of the greens and blues are still making their beds or not even out of them yet. Then even though there are over 50 tedious roles if you're in red they are going to call you out and basically belittle you, not all the guards do this, but it shouldn't be done at all. This is not the way life runs in the free or how they say it here yeah ladies you know what else doesn't happen in the free, free air conditioning, free toilet paper, free pads, free clothes, free laundry service, or a free place to lay your head down. This is merely a place for someone like me to lose all the things I worked sober for, for almost three years. I must stay positive and know that my time here will be for focusing on God. I have a daughter I was helping with her GED, I have an apartment that costs over $1300 a month, a car payment of $375, CPS which is electric that has roughly $300 a month plus groceries and toiletries and household goods. I also had to pay $300.00 a month for a scram ankle monitor for 10 months, $90.00 a month for the ignition interlock that was put into my car y'all, and I wasn't even thinking about alcohol, but God placed me here for a reason so again I digress. I guess the Lord is showing me another way some people must take to become sober. Although this was not my way, if I wanted to uplift you the reader or be a recovery coach I must have gone through these rough flocks because not everyone learns or recovers the same way. Heart hug, I actually was talking to a flock mate yesterday and don't worry I was only talking in open day room and she said this type of recovery works for her because she doesn't have a place called home and y'all that happens a lot there's a lot of homeless women in both flocks I was in so this is like heaven for them I unfortunately feel quite the opposite this feels like devil hole, the actual place I'm in but with the Holy Spirit. For me and all around me I'm able to maintain the courage and strength to learn and not judge or be bitter because as I said yes my days may be numbered here but not by anyone but the Lord my father not one Sparrow or flesh suit can change or add days or colors to my journey God has my number in my rainbow.

Blood sister

I'VE BEEN MOVED TO WRITE ABOUT MY SISTER AGAIN I KNOW I DID EARLIER when I had the dream about her in the preflock, with the house that looked the same from the outside and the truck the same but the inside was a mess with what looked like vomit from drinking, than walking in and seeing everything painted blue. Well, it's been brought to my attention that, by the Holy Spirit, I'm supposed to encourage her as well. She's my older sister by numbers and I was kind of always in her shadow, but I believe the time has come to wrap her in my arms and help her. For now, I will write about it and when I'm a free bird or feesh as we call each other, I will embrace the life out of her. I'm not sure if you have a sister big or small but love her, help her and let's do this together. Yesterday evening when I was in line to use the bathroom there's a little tree with hand cut outs by where we get water like a creative art project I used to do with toddlers but needless to say one of the hands says, Tabatha my sister doesn't spell it that way, but it's a rare name to begin with. Then right now as I'm praying and asking the Lord for heart hugs, he shows me this Mark 5:41 holding her hand he said to her Talitha kalam which means, little girl get up and the girl who was 12 years old immediately stood up and walked away. Now you may be wondering Natalie what is the point of the story but from what I'm hearing the Holy Spirit say my older sister was always the main event the star growing up she may not however have known it, but she was. Over the years she's reached to men, relationships, flesh suits and wine to comfort her anxieties depression, fear of being alone, fear of not being the best mom, or of losing her kids because of flesh suit judgment. I know without doubt she has asked for forgiveness and I by no means judge her because she's my beautiful older sister I always wanted to be like. Even when she's full of her Jesus juice wine she speaks about the Lord. What I am saying is her bones are good, but she needs to really know that her father is not of flesh. He is the Lord, the son and the Holy Spirit. We both struggled with many, many daddy issues ones far too much for this testimony. I think that we may collaborate and write a book together, so I'll keep this on task sister. Feessh, daughter of our father God, I want you to know you are enough, you are brave. I've seen you; I've heard you and I saw you go through those struggles. The good news is so did your ABBA, your dad, your father, my father walks on water. I want to be here to help you uncover your deepest flesh wounds. I think it's time for you to look up to me or should I say directly at me because we are both the same height, but in a metaphorical way let me help your shine come back. You my sister and soul sisters, do not need any substance or relationship on earth to fill up your cup. I'm here to show you through this testimony and I can't wait to hug you in person. You don't need anything but the good Lord above, not one thing did a flesh father or flesh suit say or do to you, me or you my soul sisters, mark you condemned for life. You are a daughter, child of God, you have eternal life, and you are forgiven. So put the Jesus juice or whatever form you enjoy consuming down to numb the pain. Cry it out heal, it out and let's go for a flocking Jesus run. Let's work out together like we used to be sober minded, healthy and free, like children let's live sin free in this chaotic world and things will start improving. I know this to be true and since you are reading this, I know you will see it's true as well. I can't wait to embrace my flesh sister and heart hug you soul sisters. Come on Jesus, come rescue me. We both also love listening to Jesus music. Y'all put a station on with some Lauren Daigle some Hillside some Elevation Worship even Lifehouse get some Jesus inside you. I promise it helps little at a time change your old bad habits to Jesus habits and we will get through the storms. I love you sisters, flesh, blood and soul. I went to the lady's room to get off my bunk because we could sit on our beds at 8:00 AM. I sat down and looked up and said God give me some spiritual Jesus juice, I'm reading Philippians again and wow Philippians is a good one, may God our father and the Lord Jesus Christ give you a grace and peace. Philippians 1:9 I pray that your love will overflow more and more and that you will keep on growing in knowledge and understanding for I want you to understand what really matters so that you may live pure and blameless lives until the day that Christ returns may you also be filled with the fruit of your salvation the righteousness character produced in your life by Jesus Christ for this will bring much glory and praise to God and I want you to know my dear brothers and sisters that everything that has happened to me here has helped to spread the good news for everyone here, including the whole palace guard knows that I am in chains because of Christ and because of my imprisonment most of the believers here have gained confidence and boldly speak God's message without fear.

Y'all I spoke about God the whole time at recreation without even meaning to. It was sticky out but I enjoyed my ab and arm workout and chatting while we walked on the makeshift track. I spoke to a fellow flock make about her obsession with her ex and love and going to the Bible and replacing her thoughts about him with her father, our father. She opened up a little more and smiled and laughed and I let her know I'm praying for her and I really do care and she can talk to me. This flock life is hard for people who are still deep in their addiction or beginning their recovery. I get this I love you and I am praying for you. I want to sincerely help and listen sometimes we just need to be heard now as I trickle back to the Bible story I was so deeply in before we went outside. Just reading more and more, I'll recommend that y'all read the whole book of Philippians, read the whole Bible, but for this testimony. and reasoning for empowerment and encouragement the book of John, Philippians, Romans then Matthew. Philippians 1:28 don't be intimidated in any way by your enemies this will be a sign that they will be destroyed, but that you are going to be saved even by God himself. For you have been given not only the privilege of trusting in Christ but also the privilege of suffering for him. We are in this struggle together y'all, the next part of Philippians I'm going to share is intensely goosebump giving, shine brightly for Christ dear friends you always followed my instructions when I was with you and now that I am away it is even more important. Work hard to show the results of your salvation obeying God with deep reverence and fear for God is working in you and giving you the desire and the power to do what pleases him. Can I get an Amen, have I not ladies, been saying this the whole time. Here's the best part, Philippians 2:14 do everything without complaining and arguing so that no one can criticize you, live clean innocent lives as children of God shining like bright lights in a world full of crooked people. Hold firmly to the word of God's life. That's what this testimony has been confirming this whole flocking time. At rec earlier I was looking for heart hugs like I always do outside I don't know if this was one, but it was put on my heart to share. I have a red car in the free and every car I saw parked in front of our building was red, the lady walking around has a bright red watch so I said let me see a car drive by that's red. Y'all it was a school bus but I took that as an even better heart hug because I'm here temporarily to learn and maybe that bus was the heart hug I needed to ensure I'm in the right place, but I'll be in my red car soon. A girl can wish right. I'll continue to pray and read learn and grow as the scriptures that I shared said shine bright for my fantastical love for Jesus. I can't really hide it now because like I said at rec, it just keeps pouring out of me uncontrollably which is exactly what the Lord wants for me to do. This morning confirmed that too through his word. My mom loves that song shine bright like a diamond, I'm missing my mom and our Sunday night dinners. She cooks the best food y'all, a reminder and a heart hug just now to hug, physically hug, all of your flocking family. Human touch is critical for babies to survive and as adults we really are just big babies, I need a real hug y'all it's hard to even think about because I haven't hugged my daughter in over a month or even seen her or my mom. Don't get me wrong I love all my love from my father, Jesus and his heart hugs actually squeezes, he gives me more than once a day but, a real physical hug squeeze and some happy tears sound real good about right now. I'll pray about it, I'm praying that the Lord heart hugs us now and those whom we love at home.

Knowledge in the raw

BEING IN A GROUP SETTING FOR COUNSELING IS ONE OF THE FORMS OF counseling I was trying to apprehend the concept of when I was home studying for my LCDC. Today I brought this up yet again to a gentleman who threw on a movie, short informational piece, during our group CDC training counseling session about tobacco and vaping. I enjoy these learning opportunities because I want to know the deeper thought process and traumas that influence the motives for addiction. The gentleman tried telling me again lies about myself ladies saying I was in denial over being addicted to alcohol over a poor choice I made over 3 1/2 years ago. Yes I drank and drove but I firmly 100% know I am strategically placed in this facility to gain the knowledge and wisdom, the thought processes of those who are recovering addicts. I don't like how a person who didn't read about me doesn't even know my name or my story tried to deny me of the plans the Lord clearly has for me. I guess that's the way addicts think if you're sitting with the bunch of addicts on the other end and not the LCDC counselor, not wearing a red blue or green shirt, that you are deep into some sort of addiction. Which y'all for the purposes of learning experience and learning style I will take it with a grain of salt, his thoughts about my outer appearance and position. God placed me where I am because of the connection learning and braveness he knew I would have and represent when continually told I am something or anything other than what he has called me to be. I found my purpose in here y'all I always knew I was meant to stand out, stand alone sometimes, not be in the shadow of any other. God my father knew it too, he put this light, humility, grace, love and kindness, compassion and understanding inside me long ago. He equipped me to learn how to control my tongue and anger and the judgment that he knew was coming so that I could have be brave enough to write this documentary testimony through his grace for y'all the readers. Holy heart hug as y'all read previously on the pages prior I was stuck on writing but I prayed for God to send something anything for knowledge, understanding and deeper thoughts than just praying my way home, which I'm still doing by the way God, please come rescue me from the prosecution, stones and flesh liars please hurry send that army to find me reminder, I am on bunk one in the devilcation final flock.

Brave

As I'm sitting crisscross applesauce on my blue treasure box listening to the birds chirping and cars driving by so close but so far away outside. I'm pondering on this whole experience like wow, I didn't know I could be this brave and remain compassionate and kind and obedient not only to my father but the flesh devil puppet sparrows for such a time period. This is my 7th Friday away from family and 44th day total away. My lucky number is 7 and there's that #4. At chow one of the flock mates said she didn't know why or how I was so happy in the morning, it was about 5:45 AM and I just said, which is the truth, I'm usually always in a great mood in the morning. I proceeded to say until the flesh tries to ruin it then I just put on my Jesus music and block out Satan vibes. I wanted to tell her that is also starting your day with God's word, I read my Bible before anything and also my morning

Prayers, communication with the Lord, my God chats set the tone for my day. I love knowing he listens to me in the morning, noon and night. Then we started talking about our shirt colors and the time we have left here. She too was set for 90 days but had a couple bumps on her journey and I guess got extended and put in orange a couple of times. Y'all orange is the second color of our beloved rainbow, but here it's bad. I kept thinking about my purpose here and how I am doing all I can to remain in red until I'm promoted to blue. I don't want to be demoted even though I love orange. Ladies, no matter where you are what color you are wearing be obedient to your God. Keep his commandments, I believe if I keep his commandments and believe in this truth you'll automatically fly through the places, processes, sentence, assignment that you are currently residing. God won't let you fall too long, remember Peter took his eyes off the Lord and saw the waves and devil distractions but, not for one second did God let him sink. Your God won't let you sink either girls. If you are in constant communication with him and you believe he sent his son to die for you on the cross you are saved, so keep trucking, keep the lines of communication open to him. He is for you and myself, it's going to be hard ladies it's going to be even more difficult the more you believe and the closer you get to your father because that's when the devil sends out his most powerful flesh devil puppets. But, with God, through God and for God no one can stand against you. He won't leave you for one second, right when you feel any tiny breath, word, stone or oppression from the flesh devils you close your eyes and talk to your God. Cry, beg and ask him to come protect you your family, your flock mates, your kids, y'all pray right then and there for that sparrow flesh devil puppet, judge, lawyer, or counselor that tries to disarm your God's protection. Once you believe, receive and get the knowledge and wisdom no one can take that from you. Y'all you are given eternal life by God's grace, he loves you, forgives you, protects you and equips you with mercy and faith. He is the truth, he is the life, he is the way home. Grab his hand by grabbing the Bible, imprint his words from scripture deep on your heart and soul, get a pen or a pencil or your laptop and use that flesh hand to remember, acknowledge, consume his words and actions in your life, your journey. It doesn't matter where you start, if you stumble he is always and will always come and save you. If you're hurting ask him to show you the why, then how to make it a learning Jesus moment, how to save someone else's who will be walking in your shoes tomorrow. We were given and are given this wonderful gift for free from God then when you get a heart hug, a rainbow, a red sign or an orange sign, embrace it, record it and share it. Make viral the Lord's good news, brighten someone's day by the grace and wisdom you acquired in your flock, in yourself, in your pod or in your church wherever ladies be the footprints of God your daughter can walk in right behind you. Leave a trail of wisdom and scripture to help guide them, then when something amazing happens all the glory to God who led you there and was with you all along.

Focus

I AM DIFFERENT NEITHER MORE OR LESS BETTER OR WORSE BUT I GOT AN apple at breakfast when all my other flock mates got a banana. It was clearly noticeable because it was a green apple in the mix of yellow bananas. It didn't feel like a heart hug until just now as I'm writing about it. I've been struggling since last night to connect with scripture and my words for y'all then reading the book of John verse 17 when it says he came as a witness to testify about the light, he is the light. Yall, I am not the light, because the light is God, but I highly believe I was sent to be a scripture light spreading obedient child of God, merely a vessel small vein viral flesh spreader of the goodness. I have to keep my focus on the Lord even after the flesh probation officers meetings because little by little they trickle the light out of my soul. Then it takes a couple hours to regain my spiritual energy to dive back into the Bible and the words he my father says about me. It also doesn't help that the flesh sparrows are controlled by their flesh boss ninjas and do things out of routine like asking robotic questions that are the same set and repeating the same number of days as they see written by a flesh judge PO or devil puppet. I almost don't care to have any more flesh meetings or unanswered phone call sessions because it by no means made me happy content or settled in my thoughts about the safety of my family or my daughter on the other side of these devil ordained gates. It caused me panic, worry, anxiety, fear and stole my peace my father and I have been so strategic and obedient about forming intimately together. It's hard to pray and I'm reading scripture as words with no meaning I don't like it one bit y'all. We have to retrain our thought process to know and be aware of these flesh devil appointments although they may be a part of structure and mandatory we can handle them with grace and wisdom. I prayed during them, before them and most importantly after them because at the end of the day nothing about our God has changed. He is still your control system your present, future and whipped clean your past. You are still a child of God no matter what a flesh appointment consists of remember God is and will always be working on your behalf. Girls I know first second and last hand it's hard as ever, the words being spoken seem so flesh real and condemning but, God's not done with you he is pruning you and when he's ready to set you free I can't stress it enough he has the keys to all your doors, my doors, not these flesh sparrows.

Purposeful revelation

Y'ALL I GOT TO DIRECT AND BE THE NARRATOR OF OUR PLAY HERE AT MY final flock it's a story about a mother named forgotten and her husband absent. I tried to portray it like the movie inside out with a core memory reenactment where forgotten's kids, all whom have uplifting and biblical names; faith, mercy, hope, unique, heavenly and little mystical. As I pieced together the scene in my head and wrote it out y'all it really came together fabulously. Our counselor Miss R. is reading my actual book and said I should be a director or a narrator. Y'all, ladies, when we were all done and everyone got their parts my armpits were sweaty, and I feel fantastically accomplished. I never knew I had this, taking the lead, writing the synopsis and then assigning the roles and directing in me. Well, y'all how exhilarating, although this is a low budget film I still had an awesome a assistant and a great cast.

God, I thank you for allowing me the great responsibility to direct the Mother's Day performance I also thank you for allowing my thoughts and actions to stay positive even though I still haven't been called back to make my phone call to my family nor have I received any mail from home. Instead of letting my train of thought derail and spiral down a devil hole thoughts I've been trying to redirect them and focus on the why I'm here. To uplift you the readers and my flock mates. Little do they know and even you soul sister y'all are making me brave and confident in myself to be able to explore my calling and purpose. When I get out of this flock, public speaking has never been my strong suit hence the sweaty pits, but I've gotten some feedback from my flock mates, and they said I'm crushing it. Yay, so when I get out of here, when I am rescued I will have the strength, character, endurance and wisdom from my God, the Bible to be a good news advocate, spread it through public speaking, podcasting, tik toking and most importantly this testimony, my written words through the unveiling of my purpose. What an amazing feeling y'all. Ladies don't lose hope faith or grace, use mercy and wisdom to gain access to your heavenly father and he will peel back the layers of your life's purpose through the heart breaks, the tears, the laughs, sparrows, flock mates, soul sisters, sentences, judgments and assignments he places you in strategically with a plan and his purpose for your life. That was a heart hug revelation. God continually revealing and showing us our purpose, pray about these things when they seem distorted or abstract, God answers when we he puts the places, the pieces to your puzzle back together to make it a whole production, big finale final result. The picture will be revealed, makes sense all through God who saved you, braved you and planted these seeds in you long ago. So, take root ladies we've got this, be the action behind the prayers girls.

It's the middle of the week, on my end y'all another day in the flock life it's 7:15 AM and we are racked up boxed up on freeze whatever you want to call it. I'm still praying away my anxieties and worry about the negative that keeps trying to creep into my family island memory department. I get it though ladies it's harder than ever when you know you have a child at home, when you were the sole provider and caretaker for them and you have to rely on a flesh human who has their own inequities and humanly flesh temptations that are far beyond the physical control and have been over a couple of months then when coincidentally nobody answers their cell phones at a once a month phone call from me topping it off with not receiving weekly letters as I was told I would receive as well. I get that the outside world is far busier and distracting than flock life or being locked up it just stinks when being on this side that's all we have to look forward to as far as communication from our family on the outside. I'm trying to push back the devil's constant muffles and overdrafting my bank account I've had for over 20 years, evictions, car payments not being made blower in my car being violated, Madi being in harm, something happening to my mom, my cat's not being taken care of daughter losing her home, y'all that's so much that can really derail me quick. God please take these anxieties and fears away from my thoughts so that I can keep learning and being consumed by scripture and the good news instead of devil thoughts and his vicious prowling on my brain. Ladies we got to pray for heart hugs and just keep praying for the whole situation. I'm praying for you ladies' whatever devil derailing bullhonkey thoughts that tried to creep in shut them down with the name of Jesus.

Sparrow splitting

LADIES I SWEAR THE SPARROWS ARE OUT TO GET ME. I AM NOT SURE WHAT fashion statement or hairstyle sideburns are but I have new baby hair growing in that when I put my hair in a ponytail braid or a bun the little hair stick out by my ears. A monitor, sparrow got upset with me for my flyaways being out. Y'all, I don't have hair spray or gel and they will write you up if these hairs are sticking out. It's ridiculous! I was sitting on my bed reading my Jesus cards and she started her shift yelling Chapman as she came in. Not a good start to my morning. Then she called me aside because another monitor called her yesterday at home about community service hours. A flock mate and myself already spoke to a sergeant sparrow because my flock mate had community service hours, she wanted to work towards with the dorm chores they give us. I did not get assigned any hours and I was told she could take my shift in the bathrooms. Honestly, I enjoy cleaning and mopping because I was doing it in my head for the Lord and it helps time go by. But since these burials all have poor communication with one another it got back to the ninja Sparrow in terms of me complaining or trying to play the monitors against each other period which was not the case at all. Not even remotely y'all. I enjoyed cleaning the bathrooms at least I knew and know they are really clean when I go to use them. It was just startling at 6:15 AM that a Sparrow came yelling my name with false information. They took it all the wrong way and took it to the boss sparrow ninja devil puppets. These people need to get it together that's the evil in here. I fear they are all just trying to prolong your stay here and it will be in any way possible even if it's lies and miscommunication on their parts. All I can do is continue to be obedient to the Lord and do my chores as they are assigned. Y'all I really do enjoy cleaning it gives me a sense of purpose here though you're doomed if you do and doomed if you don't. I can't control my new hair growth not their tongues I will pray for them and stay focused on the why I am here. To listen to the Lord, be obedient to him and not give light to the flesh devil puppets when they are clearly staff splitting between themselves. We were told to confront the other monitor about the situation and then got yelled at for doing so.

I am a very observant individual and I see the bullying and staff splitting being done amongst the monitors. They don't communicate correctly with each other nor have respect for one another period they will turn our flock make swords and then use our words they forged manipulated to get at each other period ladies when this happens don't fret or get upset. Be silent agreeable and apologetic. Take responsibility even when we clearly see and know what's going on. Remember God sees all things he hears all conversations if he is for you no one on this earth can be against you. My protection comes from the Lord. He will reign in and on your behalf from heaven. Trust that he will have the words to say to the sparrows when they are trying to manipulate or lie about you. I believe even if they try to write you up or prolong extend your stay just because they think they have that power and control let them have their devil thoughts and motives. Pray over them instantly. God won't leave you for a second he has the final say in your life, your sentence, and your write ups. Believe that God can and will move mountains for you girls. Part the Red Sea, serve you justice in your current state. No one has the power or control over you like the Lord. Plus once you commit yourselves to our God our father you are his. You belong to him. He won't forsake you or leave you. He's listening to all of the oppression the oppressor oppressors he's got your back and mine. Keep his commandments and his word and be obedient and he will rescue you in the midst of your storms. No flesh devil puppet sparrows right ups or stones being thrown have any authority over your life when you have a God that's all for you. Again ladies be silent don't combat with words or a fight your God already won for you. Look up pray to him and trust him. He is teaching you how to remain faithful, kind and gain wisdom and show compassion and love even when the flesh is working so hard against you. Our God is amazing and good all the time. Trust this process and love without conditions.

Appointment peace thief

ANOTHER MEAT QUEUE WITH MR. A THE PO ASSIGNED TO ME AT MY flock. I won't lie I was a little nervous because I was supposed to make my phone calls which they didn't answer but we talked about my case and the aftercare situation. All good news the numbers that's been put on his heart is still 90 him and another PO just kept telling me not to get an infraction which is written up. They also proceeded to say that this place and the sparrows are evil. Mr. a has a passion for social work status and the other gentleman just didn't seem to like it at all. I got interrupted from writing because Mondays are incredibly busy period it's now 6:35 PM and I'm finally able to finish my thoughts from this morning. Even though I had a good meeting with Mr. a my heart hurts because the flesh has confirmed my 90 days here and no letters in the mail when they said my family would write once a week and they didn't answer the phone. I'm glad I was busy cleaning and with group because now I'm sitting on my bunk and I'm sad. I know I asked for confirmation and a sign about my stay here which I got but with no answers from my family I've begun to worry if something happened to them. How can both cell phones go to voicemail.

Appointment robbed

MY HEART IS NOT SETTLED BUT I AM GOING TO PRAY THEY ARE OK IT WAS just bad timing for phone calls. God, please protect my daughter and my mom. Y'all this separation can get overwhelming at times especially because I forgot to tell you that the readers Mr.A said he ran into someone I may know she was with a gentleman, and she had a nose piercing. I was like that's my Madi bug. She was outside this dreaded building and no one told me, and I had no idea. Y'all isn't that just evil on this place's part. My daughter came to drop off items for me and I haven't seen or spoken to her in over a month and ½. No air high 5, no I love you. That right there is inhumane. I must keep it together though ladies because I'm stuck in here why does it feel more like a jail today than it has this whole time? I need to get my Bible out and start asking questions through scripture talking to the flesh hardens my heart and hurts my soul. It makes me want to bust out and cry weep and beheld still haven't had a human hug nor any human contact in far too long that's neglect I know I'm going to get through all this but it's harder today for some reason.

Plow your hardened heart

I wrote and read aloud my accountability personal inventory paper Friday the 7th 2024 during our group session here at my final flock. It lifted a heavy weight of doubt and fear and lost hope right out of my flesh heart. Reading it with a full blown tears of sorrow and remorse gave me a strength and heart hug I didn't know it was going to happen. Y'all repenting our sins and wrongdoings out loud in front of 31 strangers and God and the Holy Spirit is cleansing and exhilarating. Wow ladies who would have thunk it I feel completely awakened forgiven and humbled. It took courage, endurance, pain and humility to open my deepest wounds like I did yesterday. Ladies, if you're struggling with a doubt, anxiety and fear bring your whole bucket of worries, tears and sins to the front and center. Plow your heart and hearts before the Lord. Then love and endurance and wholeness, a harvested crop will be ahead of you. God will shower you with righteousness grace and love. All the glory to God. I feel more alive now today than I ever have. Sober forgiven and loved. Then I was able to through the Holy Spirit write my woman I want to be so gracefully and beautifully as I did. I am her. I am Natalie whom God made me to be. It feels amazing to have these thoughts about myself. I want you to experience this as well. I want you to fall in love with God the way that I have. Place all your sins and hurts at his feet. Daily, nightly plow your hearts so we can harvest our crops that the Lord will shower with righteousness and forgiveness! Y'all I also picked up a cricket, scooped him in my palms and put him outside. I've never touched a cricket alive before nor saved one's life, but it felt amazing.

Jesus in court

SUNDAY IS THE DAY OF SABBATH Y'ALL IT'S POURING DOWN RAIN OUTSIDE and our rec time has been brought to the inside. Which is normally fine but now they decided to do medication pass which means rec is interrupted by a 20 minute freeze on our lock boxes. I am praying that doesn't go against our workout time because all we do is sit on our bottoms y'all. It gave me a moment to grab my paper and pen and let y'all in on my morning session with the Lord our God our father before the 8:00 AM wake up. So yesterday in Bible study there were a lot of heart hugs but as we were saying our goodbye, they handed out a picture of Jesus in front of a judge in a courtroom. He has handcuffs on and blood all over him. I wept when I saw this and stuck it in my borrowed Bible. Then then ladies the magic happened this morning this whole time I've been praying crying rewriting the God sent his son to die on the cross for our sins. He took our sin away then there's scripture saying he wiped our sentences clean we stand trial before the Lord only. Not judges, lawyers, counselors, sparrows or devil puppets. God sent his son to die on the cross for our sins. That's exactly the Hallelujah moment I felt this morning and I pictured the picture in my treasure box between the pages of my borrowed Bible. Y'all, I had a heart hug in the holy spirit's name because I've been praying for the Lord to go into my assigned judge's heart and know who I Natalie am. That is what my shepherd my father calls me I have been forgiven of my sins. The picture came in a Holy Spirit moment because I've never seen a picture of Jesus in front of judges pew with shackles on his wrist. I started crying with words of Thanksgiving and praise to my Lord my father for showing me in such an elaborate distinct heart hug that he shed his blood for our sins. The blood is red, the red is the rescue because he sent his son to die on the cross. There's no mistaking that this was a wholly divine spiritual heart hug ladies. Even Sarah Bush the woman who I've been reading her book called "The Invitation" has these miraculous heart hugs from heaven. The Lord reigns from heaven. He will and has always forgiven you of your sins and mine. He will and has spoken to the highest authority in your life and mine. God our father is our only judge. That picture was an answer to my prayer about going into Mrs. Christine Delprado's heart and showing her what God says about me that the Lord my father had and is working on my rescue. My life and has been this whole time. Y'all isn't that a holy moly testimony. I think that is why as miss Sarah Bush speaks so highly of journaling writing these events in our lives on a tablet on our hearts. This is how we spread the good news y'all. By being obedient faithful in our prayers, fierce in the grace and hope and we are clearly being shown heart hugs and Holy Spirit signs from our father y'all. Each time you read scripture then get a heart hug write it down. Take note of how the Lord is working in our life's ladies! We all need to read, hear and see it to believe it. God is good, he is with you, and he will set you free. Just believe. Over fill your cup with Jesus juice not wine not coffee the Holy Spirit. Y'all now I read this, as a holy heart hug, after what I just wrote; but Jesus said to them immediately take courage it is I do not be afraid.

Defense attorney

Happy birthday to my beloved mom. Yep I can't celebrate her in person because I'm still trapped by the flesh. But I did just read something as always profound and amazing in my beloved Bible. On page 1631 but he forgives us completely and repeatedly the words used here are legal terms Jesus is our advocate our defense attorney in court of law who intercedes for us the lawbreakers. But he is not only the defense attorney he is also the sacrifice that atones for our sins. This means that Jesus's death has been accepted by the court as admissible payment for all of our sins. Our sentence has already been paid for by Jesus. When we bring our sins to he says he goes back to the judge his father on our behalf reminding him that our sentence has already been paid. Can I get a flocking Amen. Hallelujah! Thank you Lord, I was reminded of this by the Bible at this moment on my mom's birthday because I have no trust in the flesh system flush nothing. Not even to deliver the flush mail I wrote to my mom wishing her a happy birthday. But what I do trust is the Lord the Holy Spirit my God my father my love. I know that since I prayed to send a heart hug to my mom and a happy birthday wish he did so on my behalf. Y'all I've been nose deep into my Bible and I will say it has helped me feel loved knowledgeable and comforted knowing my father my God is working not only on my sentence but he's repairing defining himself and leading my family my daughter on his path period since they can't talk to me either they are having to turn to God to be comforted and know that I too am OK. I haven't forgot forgotten about them. I love them and I am praying for them. Yep if they love like Jesus as I do in my heart they should be diving into their bibles and trusting that the Lord will reunite all of us soon. On his time, according to his purpose for all of our lives. Wow that just made me feel at peace with not receiving any flesh mail. God has complete control over all of creation. When he thinks our people our loved ones are ready to receive flesh mail he will ensure it's delivered. Heart hugs y'all. So pray again ladies for those whom you love and may not know the love of our beloved father God yet. Remember not only is he pruning you and me he's molding the minds of the youthful changing the hearts of the hurt and healing the wounds of the world. Our God is a busy God, but he never forgets not one of us. I thank you God for showing me those scriptures and allowing me to comprehend and articulate them as I have done in your name I pray Amen.

So y'all something strange happened after I literally wrote about the mail being delivered above in this paragraph. More like received. I sent a letter out around the 21st of may to my daughter and I'll be deviled if they weren't returned to me here at this place I am currently residing. It was such a weird feeling because the sparrow thought i received a letter from home y'all i just had a bible study session with pam and spoke about placing a shield of armor and protection over our families and my daughter at home. We also spoke about the confirmations in psalms about all God's promises and being disciples of the good news and being kind and loving to everyone and passing this down to our errors our children. Also praying that our children love like Jesus pray to God trust God and are obedient to his commandments period now I'm not 100% sure what was stamped on the return envelope but I will say the devil is attacking me hard. So the sparrow calls my name and for real the whole blessed dorm is clapping with joy to come to the realization that this was in fact the letter I sent home. Not one from my daughter. Ohh boy did I get devil trumped derailed, double devil attacked Instantly. Y'all can imagine the awful assumptions I've allowed to creep into my flesh brain. I cried too, then I'm reminded of what I just wrote for y'all. Trust God! That when he's readily to confirm or deliver mail or words from flesh to whomever they will be done in his name. The Lord literally has control over the post office. Yep because I'm not second guessing the love my God has for me or the trust, I put in him or maybe there is a tiny itsy-bitsy crumb of doubt on my plate. So that return letter meant Natalie you have to let go of any doubts. And any flesh accusations worry and anxieties the flesh brings. Surrender my mail my life, my daughter to God. Bam then all those devil things that were trickling into my flesh leave instantly. Be done Satan once again I'm holding on to faith and love. God is protecting my daughter with the shield of armor while I'm in this place. I believe this is to be true. Pam the Bible study lady said she would pray for me too and she would be looking for this book, my testimony to read. Y'all this mail situation is merely a flock test of my flesh faith. God is working in us and our families and children. The Holy Spirit is in me and you and is protecting our loved ones, especially our children. He's directing the path of the mailman too. Then I wouldn't have been able to literally share what I just did with y'all. I'm patiently waiting for my God, father, abba to not only deliver my flesh mail but to receive it. When he is ready to bless and adhere to his promises he will. He always knows how much suffering we can handle. He knows our hearts he knows our thoughts. I must stop doubting even a speckle sprinkle tiny blink of an eye that my God is not good or real or that he isn't protecting my daughter and family. So you have to as well ladies. My sister, my friend we have come so far, pray away the devil thoughts and attacks. No matter what is happening in your absence of your family God will always provide. Trust him completely, don't lose faith over flush mail.

Purpose in the pain.

So ladies, I was brought from tears of missing my daughter to vicious, strong prayers being sent to move and encourage myself to trust in the Lord to come from my protection to love me and my daughter. I choose the Lord of all substances, two is better than one and three is better than two. I'm currently sitting on my little blue treasure box. Just finished proofreading the pages before this one and I'm thanking God for allowing and guiding my thoughts and prayers so gracefully to the words in this book. My heart is content, knowing that this is going to encourage you because ladies when I go back, it doesn't matter how far in the journey of these pages I'm abundantly heart hugged and moved again. Like a double whammy confirmation hug. It also doesn't matter how many times I go back and reread it or my Jesus cards it's all good news! So, I'm going to continue this day this journey with my pen and paper meetings and Jesus morning bunk talks until my father saves me. Then y'all, I know I'll be moved to collaborate with another chapter book journey of my whole life and how the world the home life is going. My daughter, my mom, my church, my family my soul sisters will be moving along with me in this journey because it's for life through Christ. Yep, no one can stop me now that the Lord has shown, proven and equipped me with my calling my brain, my experiences. Then to faithfully relay them to an audience of more than one you are reading this because it was meant to be. I'm writing it because it was God's purpose for my life to share empower, encourage and spread the good news. Ladies get a pen and paper, pencil laptop whatever and start documenting your life for Jesus. What you go through been through and future is all his plan. Someone else needs to hear feel see that it will be OK. There is purpose in the pain. Learn from our struggles and addictions our downfalls our lacking and putting all of our trust in the Lord and giving all the glory to God! Watch your bad breaks, negative thoughts, devil hole staycations transform into holy moments. Spiritually lead and moved. Heart hugs turn into human flesh hugs. Addictions and sins be forgiven and healed. Keep on swimming ladies like finding Nemo.

Just keep swimming, pray harder and louder in the darkest moments. Accept the love your father has to offer. Yall, it's free just like these pads, hygiene products and toilet paper right here right now for me. Use them all, use your prayers and your beliefs abundantly towards the Lord. He will save you he always does.

Patience in the waiting

It's a Friday on this end y'all but I don't know what day you'll be reading this so happy whatever day of the week you're at currently. It's a holiday here in Texas battle of the flowers or something along those lines. Fiesta if you will. This by no means has been a fiesta, that means a party or celebration. But the ones who put in requests to go to bed earlier and wake up later which I declined to sign, got what they wished for. We slept in, they slept until 8 and are being given privileges to sleep today for some naps. Lord help me I was up still at my normal morning meetings with the Lord. Today it was put on my heart to have more patience, as if sitting in a dark room not being able to move for four hours or sitting on my locker box for over an hour and a half while 28 flock mates shower is enough patience building. Needless to say, patience was the word put on my heart. I prayed about patience and I come to the recollection that patience builds endurance which builds character. Feels more like PTSD. But I'm trusting the process, adventure, assignment, whatever you want to call it ladies. Trust, embrace it, don't get caught up in the drama because you're bored. Be silent, be patient, be humble and kind. Pray when you feel impatient ladies trust me I know it's hard but the reward is so much better. Trust God. Y'all I'm being moved to share and tried to correctly paint a picture of some phenomenal amazing women I've met on this journey. I want to do it in the utmost respectful way as well because they have touched my soul and helped share the light and make this waterless dungeon a safe place full of the Holy Spirit. Y'all and that's hard to do I've also been moved to possibly change the title of this book testimony to the flock that braved me I originally wanted it to be the flock that saved me. Only because I know my saving comes from God, Jesus Christ, my father. These flocks have merely been the threshold or structure I've been assigned to. Built character through by learning, educating, listening to y'all. My flock mates, my soul sister. The rescue the, saving will only be from my father. But the experiences, the sisters, friendships, and even the guards and monitors, counselors, sparrows, ninjas, devil puppets those are the core of what braved me into writing and sharing this experience. This flock testimony I will do so diligently share those flock moments as they arise in my thoughts after I have asked for their permission as well. I won't be putting actual names to keep the privacy and structure over my writing legal. Heaven, forbid I overstep and end up locked up again!

Fear is a liar

LADIES, I AM SURRENDERING AND GAINING WISDOM AND KNOWLEDGE from the Bible but y'all the flesh is rotten. Lean not on your own understanding but trust in the Lord. I'm trying and praying y'all. I thought maybe writing about it would make me feel better but it's only making me more upset because it's showing me how easy it is to actually write and why is my family not even trying to comfort my flesh heart. God is seriously the only thing Holy Spirit prayer listener and prayer answer I have. I'm waiting patiently to be comforted but then it's like how long will God let my heart hurt and cry for just a tiny, I'm OK mom. Or I'm alive mom. It's hurting really bad. God hear my cries, I'll continually pray these prayers of comfort in knowing my daughter and her home and my family and cats are all safe and sound in your name Jesus. Come down from heaven and rescue me and comfort me please. I'm holding back tears because I'm trying to be strong in here and put all my trust and faith into the Lord, my father. God I trust you and I love you more than anything. Please comfort my heart. I did get a red heart after dinner chow today. There was a bright red car parked at the gate exiting these prison gates. I'll be honest my prayers on the way to chow were upset ones. Faith is believing when we can't necessarily see. It's hard to have faith when you're in a place like the one I'm currently in but overall, I know God is good and his plans for me and my daughter and family are those of good. As my flock mate Butler on her 60th birthday today just said, put my faith over my family and daughter in God's hands. And no news is usually a sign that everything is OK. There is absolutely nothing I can do but pray and hand it over to my father God. So, God take my fear and anxieties and tears and, I pray for whoever is reading this as well to be comforted in anything that they are going through.

Guard your heart

Y'ALL I JUST KEEP BEING MOVED TO RIGHT TODAY SO MY LAST PAGES
were about being derailed or deceived and lied to by Satan and his
devil puppets about my life and the answered prayers and praise I've
been communicating so diligently with my father. Then I'm reading
scripture and that's Satan wanting us to believe his lies over the truth.
It's his way of creating chaos and separation from our father and his
promises its false perception, word play devil puppets motives we must
be intentional and protect our intimacy with the Lord our God. The
scriptures say let us be on guard. Guard your heart above all else for it
determines the course of your life proverbs 4:23. Satan and his devil
puppets continually tried to tell us our prayers aren't effective, and
God is not listening or he does not care to respond. Satan will twist the
truth on who we are and tell us we are not and won't see our prayers
answered. We are not worthy, chosen, different or forgiven that's why
we must stick to the truth the way and the life for God through God.
Study the words of the Bible because just like what just happened to me
with the picture and the sparrow devil puppet trying to extend my stay
at this devilcation God already heart hugged me this morning in our
heart to heart spiritual realm prayers God's sovereignty compels us to
pray. Is there anything too hard for me God Jeremiah 32:27 do I does
he lack the strength to rescue you nothing is impossible with God Y'all
listen to this we see more fully God's light in the darkness, his goodness
triumphs over the evil devil puppets and sparrows his love covers a
multitude of sin and heals addiction his freedom releases the prisoner
his salvation delivers the loss in his life conquers death That's what the
book again I'm reading while I'm journaling and writing this testimony
is literally aligning parallel with my circumstances. I just want to say
thank you to Sara Bush for listening to his call for you to publish your
book "the invitation" it's phenomenal motivational and ladies it's merely
God's miraculous works the Holy Spirit led her to write as I am doing

for you the reader my soul sister and maybe even Sarah Bush. I love my Lord my father I pray you the reader are documenting your walk with Jesus. I want to read it I love you God and I am thankful for all you have allowed me to do with this testimony. Amen

Derailed

STOP DOUBTING AND BELIEVE JOHN 20:27 OUR PRAYERS ARE HEARD AND not forgotten this is what I read after I was derailed of my spiritual thinking and positive heart hugs that turned evil and negative due to the flesh. God is good y'all all the time believe it King John and his army were loyal to the Lord and when they were supposed to go to battle they did and the Lord kept his promise because the king general praised his name and sing songs of this this surprise attack happened and the opposing side ended up killing each other. Then, the king said the Lord has done this God has kept his promises. Y'all that's why God has called and equipped certain people in his defense to pray praise worship in our churches fellowship groups they are the frontline in our warfare those who journal write and share God's good news are moved to do so and it comes out spiritually and bravely because it's actually just God's works in our lives that we are documenting. Write it ladies, share it, flocking publish it we are here to help each other. Don't let the flesh devil puppets surprise attacks and words derail your spiritual train God did not and will not forget about you or me.

Faith

I'VE BEEN WAITING FOR A MOMENT TO BE MOVED AGAIN TO HAVE MY PEN meet the paper and here we are. I was deep into writing scriptures for y'all to eventually reference because that's how they soak into my noggin, I've been at a halt and kind of confused these past two days for some reason. I do not like it either, I felt like I was letting God down because the TV was catching my attention then y'all I did what I kept telling my fellow flock mates not to do. I drew a calendar, and I was counting my days. Y'all I can't be doing that it puts a heavy weight on my heart and pulls the blinds down on my eyeballs. Yuck I hate that feeling it brings y'all. I had my one-on-one with Mrs. R which went divine and purposeful for the Lord, I believe, but with flesh you can't ever be certain. Y'all, I handed over the 1st 140 pages of this book that was my only copy. I'm kind of having a mini panic attack I can't rewrite that it was all Holy Spirit driven and in real time. She said she would make a copy then return it to me but y'all those 140 pages are my soul so please please pray as I do as well she makes the copy then returns them to my anxious hands. This book is my testimony those pages are my soul in writing. All I can do now is pray about it the meeting went as a normal meeting would the time is still the same and yes Lord I'm trapped here in a devil hole. Even she sees the evil in here, surely God my father won't allow the suppression and condemnation for the allotted time the flesh suits are still labeling my stay. She's a holy spirit Jesus warrior too though and there was a presence and connection in that little office as well. I know my god has big plans for me and my life y'all he has bigger plans for Mrs. R too. I told her that and the devil comes to kill steal and destroy. I told her to get out of here as soon as she could. We talked about my daughter and well everything unfortunately the judicial system is discombobulated and the flesh judges are crooked. But she also believes God's her ultimate judge boss and controller. I told her I'll be praying for her, and we talked about y'all too the reader. I know this testimony is going to help and encourage you as well just the many miracles and heart hugs alone. Girls just know again even if you have a bad report,

49

bad counseling session, bad sentence cry out to your father your God and demand he come into your heart and surrender all your worry anxieties fear depression and ill thoughts to him. Do it daily, hourly, every minute. Do it as much as you need to redirect your thoughts on what he says about you. Have faith love and hope, know you're where you're meant to be may not be where you want to be but it will be better than it used to be. Take the time to write scriptures, pray and take in the air and heart hugs around you. Rome wasn't built in a day God took seven to create all around us or six rested on Sabbath, great things take time and endurance to build character. Have hope that your God has not forgot about you even if you have writer's block. Or watch a little TV or rest your hand. Your god is still working on your rescue your life your plan. God's not done with you if you're reading this if you're breathing air into your lungs god's not done with you or me have faith ladies, keep the faith in your flock.

Fours

WEDNSDAY, DAY WE MEET AGAIN Y'ALL I LOVE WAKING UP TO HEART HUGS. Not only did I have a dream about my current situation it was saying don't MTR whatever that means. Just have patience in the waiting follow the flesh suit rules and my father will rescue me. I needed this confirmation that I am right where he wants me to be. Changes won't happen unless something forces them too. I'm not saying I'm going to cause any major changes but y'all I could be a little grease on the wheel. Who knows, my father knows. It was very clear in my dream that I should not listen to any flesh suits or sparrows whom tried to lengthen or shorten my stay. The Lord is my rock my fortress my love and I woke up with a calming peace in here. Then i said lord please send me heart hugs to confirm my daughter and family are OK. I know they will appear and I will share with you all. Also not only that piece but he said don't worry keep your faith I'm going to rescue you. Y'all I wrote a lot of scriptures confirming that it won't be the judges, lawyers, counselors or paperwork. God has my sentence I am to surrender my life my situation to him daily. Block the bad news out keep the good news in and afloat. Ladies I love you and I'm here for you and so was the Lord your God. Lord please come into my life and the readers my soul sisters, flesh sisters and daughters Lord protect us guide us give us peace in the presence I trust you Lord and I love you Amen. Y'all as soon as I got done writing that heart hug in the numbers came. My daughter and I always say that commercial 444444, there's only one number to remember and that's 4. Well it came on the news channel this flock watches every morning. I was reading the scriptures, and I was writing yesterday but the volume on the TV is pretty high so it's incredibly hard to drown it out. But I'm glad because I heard the four commercial. Ladies, I'll never stop saying it it's about the little things, I still haven't spoken to my daughter or family it's going on too many days because it happened in my final flock where I am stationed currently. Y'all this isn't OK but I'm in no position to cause a fuss or ask any more questions than I already have period I'm merely listening to my father who has instructed me to be quiet, dive into scripture and not get written up. Aye captain Lord. I trust you Lord and I love you. I pray for protection over the readers myself and my family and their family Lord I thank you for waking me up on this wonderful day and allowing equipping and controlling my life and what I should be doing for you. God's timing is perfect and impeccable. He will rescue you and endurance builds character. Faith moves mountains, hope creates an atmosphere of love, let's go into this last stretch of the week with joy y'all that's how grandma would want it.

Focus on learning not the leaving

I HOPE YOU'RE ENJOYING THIS JOURNEY I'VE SO FAITHFULLY IN THE RAWEST form have been able to share with you. I'm enjoying creating an experience with you. I woke up at well 3:00 AM then I prayed like Jesus did before he walked on water and terrified a few disciples, I take those early morning wake ups to spend kind of alone time with my father before the lights, movement and noise sets in for the day. I prayed then I peed caught a good morning half awake fly by from Mrs. Brown, then fell back to a morning cat nap and resurfaced at 4:45 AM. At this morning session with my father it was put on my heart to focus on the learning and not the leaving. God is taking care of that part on my behalf, as he is taking care of your rescue as well ladies. Don't lose your hope if you've already got confirmation that you are where you belong for the time god has allotted you, look around pray and take in the whole experience. I've been being directed to not bring this book when we have groups or peer groups so I can really embrace and hear when I listen to what my flock mates are saying. That's the whole flocking point of my presence here. If you all remember I'm enrolled in the LCDC program and this is my hands on boot camp style schooling. My education if you will staycation. Y'all I don't know how you learn or if you're even at that point in your journey of life, but wisdom is in the knowledge and experiences we accept and take in. Embrace the struggle as a learning Ave. Even if it stinks to the highest or lowest levels of devil you know what there is always something to be learned, taught or heard. Another thing I'm slowly learning is to shut my mouth and listen. Ladies I know this is hard for a lot of us because for so long we were not heard, and it feels like no one is listening. God is listening and he already heard he is taking care of your journey your path he is making the way for you! Yes, you my soul sister. He is and has already written your journey, surrender your worry to him. Embrace the staycation or devilcation or if you're safely at home look around and if you're reading this it's because you were moved to make changes in power sister help a sparrow. We all need to learn love and live in this block, outside life, jail life, recovery life, rehab or wherever you live or are stationed temporarily be patient love one another hug one another and remember who your rock is your father gave his one and only son for our sins. He's made the way. Listen, silently as he directs our paths. Surrender your cares and worries and know he will rescue you from your storm. He is the judge above all else. He reigns from heaven no matter what. Again, no paperwork, no sentence, no judge, no lawyer, no counselor, no flesh suit soul can direct your life's path like Jesus. Trust the process. I also prayed a little heart hugged prayer for those red things that have been popping out in my vision path to be unfolded or revealed as well. If they are truly heart hugs then the Lord allowed me to keep focusing on them for hope of the red heart hug. At chow I saw a red cell phone, the red coffee cup and red lipstick yet again. Even though I'm wearing red it's been placed on my heart that the red is defining moment of color. So, God please send me those red heart hugs with the hope of my rescue. And ladies remember to look around, look up, look down, look everywhere for your heart hugs. Ladies, did you all know there are over 48 verses in scripture that speak on forgiveness or that act thereof? Me either I was trying to be a good Jesus lady and memorize the stories, or books in the Bible then I got sidetracked and started counting certain groups of words such as forgiveness, faith which is over 95 verses of scripture using the form or word faith. Which y'all that's spectacular if you ask me. We did have a pretty good counselor, speaker flesh suit session educate us on crystal meth which I didn't know much about. Y'all these things are scary but the more you know the easier it will be to share, relate, educate and be free of it I don't know what y'all my spirit sisters are into but I can tell you that you don't want to lose your teeth your age your skin the way this substance does. I want to empower you that if you are or aren't into whatever your DOC drug of choice is and unfortunately, it's not short for doctor that's the most slanged word in this flock. We have to create new habits and get free of this ladies. Create new healthy habits, Jesus or spiritual or buddha whatever you pray to in your universe. Do that instead of your DOC. This journey, this life is at your palms and only you can make the choice to put it down. Then the work comes in after your choice to put it down. Be sober and start your recovery journey which lasts your lifetime. Yep, this is a choice and a lifestyle that you will have to make every day. But y'all, there is no other way than free of sin, natural highs you get from loving your kids and watching them grow and being a part of a healthy positive community in society. I know this to be 100% the truth. I know also deep down in your heart you just want to be loved the way you love, heard, treasured and respected. So, respect that God knows this, and he forgives he. Then have faith and hope and gain wisdom through learning the scriptures that repeatedly confirm this to you. All that should be in your palms and not your DOC. Let's take that acronym and make it something positive ladies. Dreams of choice, days of change, director of character! Seriously we can do whatever the Lord puts in our hearts I know this to be true if you're reading this ladies. That means gaining the knowledge, making the changes, believing, trusting then sharing the good news the it works out for good through Jesus Christ favor with grace and humility. I will continue to focus on learning from my passion and love for my father so I can hurry up and get this holy moly testimony in your palms. Girls, ladies, I love you and I don't know you, but I love you and God loves you. Put that DOC down in the name of the Holy Spirit and let's change lives.

Box sits / Jesus Juice

· ·

It's THURSDAY ON MY SIDE OF THE PAGES MAY 2ND IN 2024 TO BE EXACT. It's 6:15 AM and I've had a bit of not writers block but the actual noise and distractions around me have been clouding my time with my father, God and the Holy Spirit. I'm still very much in communication with him and the Holy Spirit is present. Sometimes I feel distracted and don't have a specific moment I wanted to write or share. On the way to chow I continually pray for my rescue and for the protection of my family. As we get back this morning the TV is turned on and as usual is loud and negative sounds voices and news. It was placed on my heart to open my Bible and, manage my time, is the portion of scriptures that I'm called to read and consume as my spiritual juice for the day. Time management is big in here which is strange because we spend more time on our boxes, eating, showering and watching TV than any other beneficial activities towards positive improvement. I'm not losing faith in my father, but I fear the time here trying to partake in the flesh activities is causing a halt in the learning department. I'm going to have to steal my mind and drown out the voices, noises, TV and food consumption and have blinders on while I dive deep into my Bible. Proverbs 28; 20 the faithful will abound with blessings those who trust in their own wits are fools; But those who walk in wisdom come through safely. Proverbs 29:2 when the righteous are in authority the people rejoice; But when the wicked rule the people groan. Y'all I'm trying really hard to find some comfort in the time I am here, but it's been hard today. As I stated earlier this morning it's like there's a roadblock from knowledge. As I'm rereading those scriptures, I wrote I am trying to remain faithful to my father, I need a heart hug it feels like.

There is a new flock mate with my daughter's name, but that just makes me miss her even more. I'll take it as a heart hug though. Then it's true about righteous people being in authority and us rejoicing because we were just as a whole flock speaking about how certain sparrows, devil puppets are just on a power control manipulative streak and could care less about integrity or human rights or even dignity for that matter. It's sad y'all. Plus, today is Thursday which means no outside recreation. This saddens my heart. These weeks are supposed to be going by faster per what the flock mates say but the structure is so discombobulated in this flock life there's not much knowledge, growth, love, kindness or dignity at all in this devilcation. I'm going to keep praying for my God, my father my ABBA to come rescue me ASAP. I've watched the process of the intakes to the ones being discharged and how you go through your sentence, what the judge says, to what your PO says to your appointed counselors, then the monitors who can write you up and extend your stay and the paperwork and communication that us at this place as residents have no say in the process. So, when you don't ever see a PO and your counselor isn't at work you're basically only left with the prayers to your God. I know and trust that no matter what the intake and discharge fleshly human process is, I Natalie, will be taking care of by my father God and the Holy Spirit through the whole process through my plans that the Lord has set for me. Regardless of what the flesh and paperwork say, my God, my father has my process, y'all when I shower, I now think about washing my God's feet my father my daughters and my moms and my families. All for the Lord. Then after I scrubbed my own toes for the Lord, a fire or combat jet flew over as as soon as I sat on my box to dry my feet. Heart hugged that my God my father is working on my rescue still and will while I'm sitting somewhat confused and at a knowledge block. Keep praying ladies he's still working on it.

Jesus is my jam

RED HEART HUGS Y'ALL, IT'S SATURDAY AND THE WEEKENDS HERE ARE SO different and slow compared to the weekdays. I'll admit I've caught wind of the TV watchers I even prayed about it because I felt like something I was doing was unproductive and wrong. There was a movie on but y'all it's OK for me to take a break from writing my book and being submerged in the Bible. So don't be so hard on yourselves either ladies. I kept thinking if I don't stay nose the Bible God isn't going to be working on my rescue. That's not true at all. If our hearts are in the right place, for God we can surrender our worries, self-judgments and cares to the Lord. Live in and for the moment as long as you're living for God. Then we had ran over on the time of our showers and some had to take them after chow lunch, me and it ran into the time that the cute Bible study ladies come in. Again, I felt like I wasn't being a good daughter to the Lord. I asked the girls that got to attend, and they said it was amazing as always and it's awesome that they missed me in there because they know Jesus is my jam. They talked about the apostle Paul. Which is a hard hug because they said even when Paul was trying to be obedient to the Lord and no one believed him. Then one of my flock mates did a walk by chat and said because she's a light like myself we don't have to prove anything or say or show because when we have the light and god's love in you and for you it shows. No matter if you show up for a Bible study take a little break from the Bible. The good news is then spread when they say hey Chapman we missed you in the Bible study. They noticed a light was missing. Then when Pam the Bible study lady came out, she gave me a red journal. Yep, heart hugging the red. She even noticed her remembered me y'all God is good all the time. So even if you, ladies miss church or watch a movie with your kids God is still with you and working on your rescue. Keep believing, keep praying and spreading the good news. Thank your God for every little, big, loud or silent whisper heart hug y'all. Heart hugs in the red.

Good news

It's Sunday y'all and today has been a glorious good day. I had a wonderful conversation or prayer if you will with my father this morning and every time I go to chow and now when I shower I wash my feet. I feel so close to the Lord and know the Holy Spirit is definitely in this place I currently reside with my flock mates. Ladies I also ran today at recreation and I usually have a hard time with running because I feel like my lungs must work too hard but today a flock mate became not only one of my favorites, but us also both being a libra and Jesus card users but running motivation. It was exhilarating if you know me again, I can walk all day long, but running has never been a thing, now it is. And she's been sharing her life story with me and our love for the Lord and the Bible. It's a divine friendship y'all. I've been praying for a lot of my flock mates here when I have conversations with them because prayer works. We all need to feel loved, valued and heard. I feel like it's one of my divine duties to add specific prayers about my fellow flock mates. We must lift each other up keep each other's heads above the waters of a devil sink hole. There is an evil in this place but together as believers of God and followers of Christ and learners of his word we can keep the light in here while we work through our own individual assignments. Ladies, soul sisters, friends we have to empower each other. That's what we'll spread the good news. Turn someone's day around even if you don't feel 100% happy yourself. The other flock mate might have just what you need to brighten your day. If we are all working on lifting one another up and seeing the positives and learning through the pain and sadness they can conquer each day together that the Lord has put us here on. Days may still be rough, but a smile, a run, a conversation could be just what God ordered. Gain the wisdom and grace and love and honor our father has put right in our hands, minds, bodies and souls and let's unleash the good. Fight evil together.

Inside out

Y'ALL I'VE SEEN THIS MOVIE BEFORE WITH MY DAUGHTER AND HER COUSINS but watching it this time around for some reason hit me different. It's actually a very well-constructed representation in animation of emotions and memories, all the little innuendos like derailing train of thought train and how sadness sometimes has to come front and center before joy, anger, fear and disgust. I cried because I realized how important your core memories are in your development and my daughter have been through a lot. I can't wait to get out of this flock and communicate all this knowledge and wisdom I've discovered here to help her deal with what she may be going through as a team y'all that's the most important reason for educating yourself about the Lord and about your emotions and core values and memories that's the foundation of Jesus like life and soul wisdom is knowledge it speaks about this in the Bible over and over I love this movie ladies and if you haven't seen it you should watch it with your kids it's got adult humor and representation as well as laughs for the younger ones plus it really pulls your heartstrings if you're a mob parent aunt to know how important our actions are in our baby's lives. I've been searching for my heart hugs today high and low I currently only really tapping into the ones that appear in the morning during my talks with God. There was a semi parked outside during rec that was red and now the Wizard of Oz is on and her shoes are red. She says there's no place like home there's no place like home so ladies maybe I just had another heart hug again I'm unclear of what the red represents thus far but I'm hanging on to hope that it's connected to my departure or exit from this flock. I believe or feel reddish for my savings so I'm writing out the red heart hugged again. I'm still formulating my thoughts on how I want to represent my flock mates probably as a whole. Kind of like a written group counseling session, perhaps y'all in the Wizard of Oz talks about somewhere over the rainbow. Heart hug squeezed and loved. Lord I love you and I trust you and I would love for you to come into my heart and whoever is reading this and heart hug us all day long. Writing that gave me a sense of peace and calmness, I'm praying for you ladies in hopes you cling on to the patience during the wait of your rescue. God doesn't make promises he won't fulfill. If you just believe and listen to your control system God will save you no matter how broken the buttons are. Y'all as i'm watching this movie i got two more red heart hugs, the puff of smoke the witch goes away with is red then the first horse when they get off at oz is red. Heart hugged again. The lion's little bow and his hair is red as well and the gargoyles wings have a red lining. OK y'all I just got abundantly heart hugged with red. Every time this happens, we have to pray and think our father our Lord and our savior. I trust you Lord I'm trying to be patient in the waiting for our rescue. The sand in the hourglasses red y'all my hope faith and love is heart hugged confirmed in red. Ladies take the time to look around for the small things the birds eating worms, the cat tiptoeing across the field, all the foods your daughter or child would eat that you left on your plate. The fighter jets flying across, the two white flowers in a field of yellow, the Ruby red slippers. Focus on them because then when something amazing, unexplainable, unimaginable to the flesh eye or soul happens you can then go back and give all the glory to God. The Holy Spirit. The one- and only-way truth and life. Plus, y'all it's easier on your soul to look for positives than see all the negative around you that may be out of your physical flesh control.

Sobriety is forever

As I was having my morning prayer conversations with my father in the dark on bunk #1 where I have been residing for the past too many days, but whose counting, I was struggling to find peace and hope. I cried a little and the words from Wizard of Oz were playing in my head. There's no place like home, and somewhere over the rainbow. Y'all I couldn't get comfortable with this whole not hearing Madi's voice or getting a letter from her. I'm really trying to favor the saying no news is good news but when I have all this downtime to get derailed from my train of thought, I begin to think, abstract, out-of-the-box, way out like inside out with Bing bong. If y'all haven't seen it that's riley's imaginary friend as a young child. I know my thinking and prayers were going on a looney loop so I asked the Lord to let me sleep for a couple more hours without a bad dream. Then I had a dream I was in a facility like the one I am but better because the healing animals and Family Day. Before I traveled to my final flock I got news of a close friend slipping in their own sobriety journey. I feared this especially because I am in no way shape or form to be able to even communicate with them. Y'all this is a feeling I can't describe because when you are locked away there is absolutely no form of communication that can be done except for prayer. It's wild to think that this person was out in the free world while I'm here locked up And they're the one with the addiction problem. But God has bigger plans for us ladies we have to hold on to his way his will his truth. In sobriety being honest with yourself and asking for help from God our father is sometimes a hard task. It takes humility braveness and a brain and a heart just like the Wizard of Oz had promised each character. If you've watched the movie little did the scarecrow, tin man and lion know they had what they were asking for the whole time already inside them. The dream unfortunately ended with an argument with the addicted friend in the free world. Ladies the Lord's plans for us are definitely sober ones. Ones of encouraging others and going through recovery sober for whatever length of time the Lord allows our time on earth. So then my thoughts started going towards yes the Lord my father your father is in control of you me your friends your family all of us. Just like the Control Center in inside out showed up frames from the father and mother's perspectives. We are all in this together as a family. And I feel heart hugged.

Shine bright for Jesus

· ·

PHILIPPIANS 1: 28 DON'T BE INTIMIDATED IN ANY WAY BY YOUR ENEMIES this will be a sign to them that they will be destroyed but that you are going to be saved even by God himself. 29:For you have been given not only the privilege of trusting in Christ but also the privilege of suffering for him. 30: We are in this struggle together. Y'all the next part of Philippians I'm going to share is flocking goosebump giving. Philippians 2:12 Shine brightly for Christ dear friends you always followed my instructions when I was with you and now that I am away it is even more important. work hard to show the results of your salvation, obeying God with deep reverence and fear. 13 for God is it working in you giving you the desire and the power to do what pleases him. Can I get an Amen y'all. Have I not ladies been saying this whole time here is the best part. Philippians 2:14 do everything without complaining and arguing. 15 so that no one can antagonize you live clean innocent lives as children of God shining like bright lights in a world full of crooked people. 16 hold firmly to the word of God, life that's what this testimony has been confirming this whole time. At recreation earlier because it's now 10:15 AM I was looking for heart hugs like I always do outside. I don't know if this was one but it was put on my heart to share. I have a red car in the free and every car I saw parked in front of our building was red. Yep. The lady walking around has a bright red watch so I said let me see a car drive by that's red. Y'all nope it was a school bus but i took that as an even better heart hug because i am temporarily here to learn and maybe the bus was the heart hug I needed to ensure I am in the right place but I'll be in my red car soon. Haha a girl can wish right. But it was a nice confusing heart hug. I wasn't too sure about the red cars or bracelet but I'll continue to pray and read. Learn and grow as the scriptures that I shared said shine for my fantastical love for Jesus. I can't really hide it now because like I said it wreck it just keeps pouring out of me uncontrollably period. Which is exactly what the lord wants for me to do this morning confirmed that 2-3 and four fold through his word. My mom loves that song shine bright like a diamond. I'm missing my mom and our Sunday night dinners. She cooks the best food y'all. A reminder and heart hug just now to hug physically hug all of your family. Human touch is critical for babies to survive and us as adults really are just big babies. I need a real hug y'all. It's hard to even think about because I haven't hugged my daughter in over a month or even seeing her or my mom. Don't get me wrong i love all my love from my father Jesus and his heart hugs actually squeezes he gives me more than once a day but a real physical hug, squeeze and some happy tears sound real good about now. I'll pray about it, i'm praying that the lord heart hugs us now and those whom we love at home.

Numbered differently

As I'm reading my Bible and praying and crying over in the back corner sitting on my blue Treasure box I looked in front of me to see that I am an outsider from this flock. Not better not worse just different. I'm in constant communication with my Lord my father because I know 100 times Infinity he is the only way truth in life. Seeing all these ladies in the chairs watching TV made me feel a weird sadness. I wish I could counsel these ladies outside of here be their go to recovery coach because they see me as one of them. They can trust me I do not judge. Our flesh suits are made to judge but I can honestly say I've humbled myself to never judge anyone a long time ago because y'all you never know what someone has been through or what they're going through right now. I want to only make people feel happy and get their shine for Jesus either started or back or maintain it. I want to meet people who think like me from my church. I want to load up my red car with my mom and my daughter and bring them to church then have a fantastical family Sunday with good food from my mom's cooking and good company and conversations. I want this book to get out there already because our days are numbered on this earth, by our father not the sparrows.

The best is yet to come

PHILIPPIANS 3:8 YES EVERYTHING ELSE IS WORTHLESS BECAUSE WHEN compared with the infinite value of knowing Christ Jesus my Lord. For his sake I have discarded everything else counting it all as garbage, so that I can gain Christ; 9 and become one with him. Heart hug y'all. I literally came to this flock and the last one with only the clothes on my back this flock that minus my shoelaces and this book. It continues to read I no longer count on my own righteousness through obeying the law rather I become righteous through faith in Christ. For God's way of making us right with himself depends on faith. The best is yet to come y'all. I literally just had the best start to the counseling part of this facility. Mrs. R we will call her is sent from God. She's a Holy Spirit warrior like myself. I can't wait to write after our group, a one-on-one tomorrow. You the reader won't know how long of a pause that was between writing but group counseling lasts from 1:00 to 4:00 PM. Then we have to rack up and get ready for chow at 4:15. Then we walked back with full tummies once again you know I didn't eat the bread y'all, but I want to reintroduce my counselor Mrs. R. I didn't really know what to expect but our good peer group trickled into a phenomenal group council session. First let me retract and tell you what I said would ask the question tell us about one of the best most exciting times in your life. Well ladies, like he's done this whole time the Holy Spirit came into my soul and when it was my turn, I merely said the best is yet to come. Actually, I'll go deeper I said obviously having my daughter but besides that I know the best is yet to come when I publish this testimony and help empower and touch people's lives. The Lord has placed this on my heart and I cannot stress this enough. That was a heart hug session. Then when we went to Mrs. R she felt and brought a good presence with her period she was beautiful and vibrant and I could tell she has the Holy Spirit in her too. Y'all she also has a heart tattoo on her left foot that looks like it could resemble the one in my cross on my wrist. I'll have to ask at my one-on-one but y'all when she asked how we were feeling I was moved to speak after she said something about believing in a higher power for your recovery and I know she was talking about our God. She had cute jellies on her feet and she had a Kitty that imprinted on her and passed away, but all the heart hug connections were divine and holy. She's been through a lot as well, but I know I felt an instant connection to her and her to be my voice and she is going to actually listen to me. And hear me. She made eye contact with me and the others and I know she cares. I told her about this book and testimony and I also let her know she would be the first to read it. Asking you shall receive seeking you will find. I was praying all morning if y'all remember and a lot of what I wrote was about learning and ohh, reminds me another school bus was going by when we walk back from dinner chow. Gotta mean something maybe miss frizzle from the magic school bus is going to be the one taking me home. I digress, back to heart hugs and speaking about my father my Lord and savior rolls off my lips like lyrics to my soul. It comes naturally. I never knew I could express my love for Jesus so edumacated. Again ladies I know that's not the way you spell it but this is my testimony and I can cry if I want to or misspell words y'all. Each time I walk to child I'm still praying and singing the rescue song and saying God I trust you and I love you. Ladies if you ever need to redirect your thoughts that's the ticket create a healthy tune and silent if you have to because I have to remain mute. But regardless of whatever circumstances you're in say I love you. God, I trust you God I know the plans you have for me are good. It really works even if a flesh soul starts spitting out bull hockey don't disrespect them just remain externally calm while you talk to your father. He is the only one the truth the life and the way the path he has the keys to open your doors and mine and he calls you by name. Heart hug I was just thinking this place doesn't even know my real name. They call me by my last name but my name is Natalie. The Lord calls me by that name and daughter. He knows the hairs on our head lady's soul sisters he did not make a mistake. Only your father can number your days. I must constantly remind myself of this due to the flesh suits, the sparrows putting numbered labels and colors by which a game I am not interested in playing. I dig deeper into my Bible when I start overthinking about poor me why am I here. Woman up, Natalie you're here to heal some souls and yourself. Spread the good news be a light in someone's darkness. I hope this book finds its way into this flock's hands and my pre flocks. How flocking great would that be. I don't want to write unless I'm prompted by the holy spirit so I'm going to have to open my bible and get some guidance. I love you ladies remember to smile sometimes your smile alone could be just what someone else needed.

Habits

WE SMILED AT EACH OTHER BECAUSE THAT'S ALL WE CAN DO IN HERE. Y'all might remember my side bunky in my preflock because she celebrated her 44th birthday with the intense shakedown on 4/11 2024. She just came out of another room and we made direct eye contact. I knew she would be here soon that means she passed her GED test and I told her she would be coming here to this flock. I prayed for her and here she is. What a heart hug memory. She had a wonderful spirit and I would always share my commissary with her period I pray she gets to read my book because she is now a character mentioned twice. I knew the number 4 was the only number to remember. John 11: 44 so the dead man came out bound hand and foot with linen strips and his face wrapped in a handkerchief Jesus said to lose him and let him go. I spoke about the 44th b-day as well. Happy Thursday y'all or whatever day you are reading this. I woke up before 5 as always and got to brush my teeth in silence. Today is my 7th day here and 30th day total in this flock. The Lord put it on my heart to say this, that's the 30 days it takes to make or break a habit. Y'all my habit my way of life is through Jesus Christ my lord my savior i will be obedient to him no matter where I am in life this I know.

Infinity love

ANY OTHER LOVE I COULD KNOW. I FEEL AT PEACE RIGHT NOW AND comfort waiting patiently for my rescue. In the waiting I will document all these learnings and heart hugs from scripture. Yall I feel so lucky to feel this way given my circumstances. If y'all could physically see me you would think everything but I'm sitting on a hard blue treasure chest away from home hairy, but clean, tired from the flush suits but in love and content that my father. The Holy Spirit is and has been phenomenally wonderful to me and through me. I hope and pray you too feel these feelings of joy, peace and love. I'm going to pray my way out of here and through here. I really want to find that story about when Jesus said roll up your bed in the middle of the night. The whole part of Romans is fantastic y'all I can't copy all of it but I will add some reference scriptures in the back of this book. As I was looking for the story I didn't find it but I said in my head for where your treasure is so there your heart will be. Not that this blue treasure box thing is my personal treasure chest, but it holds this Bible and my book to you the reader with my deepest heart testimony. So that's a kind of heart hug. My back is really starting to hurt today y'all i can't wait to be rescued and actually sleep in a bed that has a mattress and pillows. I'm getting too old for a flat floor like top bunk. But I'm grateful I have a safe place to lay my head at night. I know my father is for sure not going to let me, his daughter suffer too much longer. I kind of feel like the sparrows and flesh mates are catching wind of my spirit. They can control my physical movements and say things to try and crush me, but my father will save me from this flock. They won't be able to stop it or persecute me any longer. Y'all won't know how long of a pen break I take but I need one. Till pen meets paper again audios. I watched the part of the movie that's on called the son of God which is Jesus dying on the cross and there's a rainbow in the scene after he dies on the cross and asks for water, a slight rainbow appears in a circle around the cross, that is a heart hug y'all. Rainbow style. That brought my love for rainbows back to the surface. Then I started crying when the song

Mary did you know came on because it says he walked on water. Y'all, I love the Lord the son Jesus and the Holy Spirit. Thank you, Lord, for showing me all this before bedtime I need to have sweet dreams. Ladies take some deep time tonight before you lay your head down and pray the devil out of your situation. He's listening, he loves you and me. All these things I've been writing about and prayers and words, epiphanies are directly from the Holy Spirit. I literally sit back and close my eyes and meditate on the word and God then, bam a heart hug. Remember too ladies I know you may be in a place where you may clearly not want to be or maybe you know deep down you're right where you need to be or maybe you had judges, lawyers, parents, boyfriends, sisters, brothers or grandparents or any flesh suit falsely accuse or misrepresent you. I wrote about that in previous chapters, let them. Be locked up for the words you'll use if you believe in God your father will come from the holy spirit. Trust that he will guide you through the storm. There will still be rain, pain, sorrow, loneliness, thunder and lightning but if you take his hand and allow him to fill up your heart and your cup you will get through whatever he puts in front of you. Look how far I've come. I don't know your journey or where you are in your walk with God but even if you start today ladies, he already knows you, every strand of your hair, he knew your name and he has already made a plan for your life. Listen, follow and love. But most importantly don't stop believing. Even when the judges, lawyers, flesh suits, sparrows, devils puppets try to haunt deceive and condemn you pray for them love them and grab his hand. Hold that bible and dig into it. Reread what you don't understand and ask God to dummy it up for you. He does it for me he knows how you learn two. He knew you before you were created. He is the truth the way and the life. Plus ladies take a look at what you're going through whether good or bad at this moment and if you think it could help someone share it. The good, the bad and the ugly. You are not ugly you are beautiful, brave and strong that's why you picked up this book because maybe a flock saved you. Maybe you'll save a flock, maybe we can help save sparrows who knows. Yep, I did that on purpose, but seriously you may just be the story someone needs to hear for their own recovery, abuse, addiction, judgment or just a light in someone's darkness. I want to add a little glitter to your darkness. Sparkle to the rain, rainbow to your storm.

I hope you sleep well tonight and if you're reading this in the morning I hope you enjoy your coffee and have a wonderful day, or if you're well, wherever you are or whatever you're doing it in the glory of your father who walks on water y'all.

Bible thumper

Y'ALL, I WENT TO THE LADIES ROOM THEN GOT ON MY BUNK BECAUSE WE could sit on our beds until 8:00 AM. I sat down and looked up and said God give me some spiritual Jesus juice. I'm reading Philippians again and wow Philippians 1: 2 may God our father and the Lord Jesus Christ give you grace and peace. 1: 9 I pray that your love will overflow more and more and that you will keep on growing in knowledge and understanding. 10 for I want you to understand what really matters so that you may live pure and blameless lives until the day of Christ's return. May you always be filled with the fruit of your salvation the righteous character produced in your life by Jesus Christ for this will bring much glory and praise to God. One: 2 and I want you to know my dear brothers and sisters that everything that has happened to me here has helped to spread the good news. 13 for everyone here including the whole palace guard knows that I am in chains because of Christ. 14 and because of my imprisonment most of the believers here have gained confidence and boldly speak God's message without fear. 15 it's true that some of our preaching out of jealousy and rivalry. But others preach about Christ with pure motives. 16 they preach because they love me for, they know i have been appointed to defend the good news. 17 those others do not have pure motives as they preach about Christ they preach with selfish ambition no sincerely intending to make my chains more painful to me. 18 but that does not matter whether their motives are false or genuine about Christ is being preached either way so I rejoice. And I will continue to rejoice. Y'all I spoke about God the whole time at rec without even meaning to. It was sticky out but i enjoyed the AB and arm workout and chatting while we walked on the makeshift track. I spoke to a fellow flock mate about her obsession with her ex and love and going to the bible and replacing her thoughts about him with the father the lord. She opened up a little bit more and smiled and laughed and i let her know I'm praying for her and I really do care and she could talk to me. This flock life is hard for people who are still deep in their addiction or beginning their recovery. I get it I love you and I'm praying for you I want to sincerely help and listen because sometimes we just need to be heard period now as I trickle back to the Bible story I was so deeply in before we went outside. Just reading more and more i'll recommend that you'll read the whole book of Philippians well y'all read the whole bible but for this testimony and reasoning, for empowerment and encouragement the book of John, Philippians Romans than Matthew.

Chores for the Lord

. . . .

WE ARE DOING DORM CHORES ON SUNDAY AT 1:10 PM AND YEP Y'ALL already know I'm going to mop and squeeze and pray to my God and sing those scriptures. I'll be back in a jiffy. It took me 15 minutes to mop this whole area y'all I feel good and energized. I wish I was in the out now so I could do chores with my daughter. That was a heart hug too. We loved working together cleaning together. I miss helping her organize her room and closet. Spring cleaning if you will. I pray she keeps up the house while I'm away again y'all it's the little things. The cleaning things that just being in someone's presence things those are what mean the world when they are abruptly taken away from you. So, ladies hug your people love your people clean with your people pray with your people and just be in the moment with your people. Put the phones down, social media and TV's and be present in the moments because I'll tell you it stinks when the flesh takes that away from you. Even just the sun on your face and the birds chirping. Take it all in while you mop while you do laundry while you walk outside. Those are all big things, grab a hug whenever you can, this no hugs for so long is inhumane. Those who gloat over my suffering is a Psalm I just heard the guard whom doesn't really like me say. Meanies. Y'all it's 5:30 PM on Sunday and we already ate another meal. I dislike fake McRib meat. Anywho, I'm sitting here trying to think about what comes next in this flock life journey. I completed the schedule because now it repeats the same every day of the week. The TV is turned back on, and I highlighted where the TV is on y'all they watch TV 90% of the time in here. It's already been on for almost three hours today and we already cleaned so it will be on from now until 9:00 PM this evening. Why on God's green planet do we watch TV on the weekends yet aren't allowed to make a phone call to our family. My family is hopefully doing what we always did and eating dinner together at my mom's apartment. I pray they are keeping this tradition alive for the sake of my daughter and all of them because they need each other. I need them. This has been such a long drawn out assignment but I'm sticking to my prayers and heart hugs.

This testimony this book, is coming together pristine in God's timing on everything. So I'm going to take a pen break read some Bible and finish the other workbook they gave but don't ever check. I'm praying for you ladies I'm praying for you your family your flock my family my flock. Tell God I trust you I love you I surrender my worry.

Integrity

DOING THE RIGHT THING EVEN WHEN YOU DON'T THINK THAT ANYONE is watching. That's what action was being taken at 4:30 AM on this Monday. The guard sparrow was waiting for one of the elderly ladies with a chair to wheel her back to her area. Y'all, she did that out of kindness and empathy and compassion. It was a great way to wake up instead of yesterday's sparrows with the rules. Then I lay there until 5:00 AM having, y'all already know, my morning chats with my lord integrity was the first word that popped into my head. Then the Lord put it on me to get excited about my new schedule with my family. That's why I was writing the schedule but on Sunday that was the last one the schedule now repeats for the duration that you are here. God put it on my heart to invest some time today in my home schedule to ensure success for my family. It gave me excitement y'all looking forward to my future at home. Sharing all these epiphanies, knowledge in Jesus time.Now the guard just saying there is power in the name of Jesus break every chain. I love that song ladies. Goodness, thank you for all these morning heart hugs. I also thought about going on my morning walks with Jesus. Coffee with Jesus and typing this for Jesus. I literally can't wait. This morning I surrender all my worries and anxieties and will focus on my future. Y'all need to do the same. I love you Lord and I trust you.

Growing in grace

As I'm reading my Jesus cards on grace, it was pointed out to me that growing in grace is the way God changes us. It allows God to accomplish in us and our children and family what we cannot do ourselves. Reading that letter I received from my daughter confirmed that by God removing me temporarily from her life is and was his plan to work in her and accomplish his plans for her as well. God is so fabulously good y'all. We have to continue to pray and praise his good news his name it's our greatest responsibility as parents and grandparents to pray for our kiddos and family. This separation from my daughter was just what she needed to be able to see and know what integrity, patience, humble, humility and faith is. We can as parents continue to have hope and faith in God to answer our kids prayers as well as ours. Looking back at the big picture this was all done for good. To help pave the way to spreading the good news in a way for everyone's learning style to confirm and not only learn but believe that this is all because of God. All the glory all the praise will be to him alone. We as humans stay obedient and listen to his direction and he will conduct our paths. He won't forget about the caboose or the conductors roles. No derailing with the Lord. Sometimes like inside out when Riley had to feel the sadness for family, then joy is back in the picture when the family is brought back together. Our lives are always changing but we have to trust that God is directing our paths y'all. Document, document, document it. I can't wait to do that podcast with Madi spreading the good news of the Lord our father. Sharing this book and spreading the good news with every Ave. possible. Like it says too in the Bible on top of houses. Now y'all we have so much access to be viral about our lives and we should be using it to spread God's love and truth. Empower, encourage and brave all those around you. Just listening to the news they put on here in devilcation, final flock is bad news. It causes depression, anxiety and fear. If we just took a moment to be intimate with our father our God who gave us life, eternal life, listen, read and gain grace and wisdom from the bible the world would become a better place.

42 Jesus streaks

THIS IS MY 42ND DAY AWAY FROM MY DAUGHTER AND FAMILY. THIS IS THE 19th day of not hearing her or my family's voices. But y'all this is my 42nd day of talking to my father, my best friend, my love, my conductor, my judge and his son Jesus Christ. This is the 42nd day of being deeply connected and rooted in the words of the Bible and being intimate with my savior. My 42nd day of praise and deep prayer and closing it with his name. 42 days of loving trusting and being obedient in what he is calling me to do. Not only 42 days of falling more in love with my God but 177 pages of his, by his grace, honor and power, documenting and sharing the good news in scriptures on my Jesus card and these pages. Something I had no idea was inside me. It's not a sixth sense like my original thoughts had advised me y'all, it's the Holy Spirit. This book is conducted, conformed, confirmed, articulated all because God and the son of God, Jesus Christ allowed me and penmanship to produce this for you. By the glory of God this book will change us. It's pointing straight to God through the scripture by the experiences and from the acquired knowledge of the Bible. God is good all the time y'all.

Fly free

RED CARDINALS WERE SEARCHING FOR WORMS IN THE TALL GRASS WHEN we walked towards the trees where we placed our outside mats at during our outside recreation today. Yep there were two of them singing and playing in the free open sky. Why they decided to fly inside these razor sharp barbed wired fences is beyond me. If I was a bird free to roam the skies places of danger would be all that I would be avoiding. Needless to say heart hugging the red y'all. This is my last Friday in the color red shirt that I've been wearing for over 40 days. I prayed last night and while this whole time that if my rescue is in red for God, as he's showed me signs to glide on with the wet and dry cloth, to show me red heart hugs to confirm my rescue is in the red. Y'all I'm receiving the heart hugs, the red scrubs the nurse was wearing, the red Cardinals flying free and the bright red sunrise. All the red cars that catch my eyes, the red exit sign inside our dorm. All of which seem to be God confirming the rescue is in red but my flesh is still in denial. It doesn't seem humanly possible for anyone to escape this place in red nor until the flesh suits deem your stay here over with paperwork and a certificate. That is the flesh though. God's will and plans are what ultimately matter. He has the final say, he reigns from heaven. He can send his angels from heaven to rescue anyone and make anything happen. I will hold on to faith, hope and my God's words and will for my life. Even the words of the Bible are confirming what the Holy Spirit is showing me, but my flesh eyes and flesh heart are stubborn. Sometimes seeing is believing but faith is believing without seeing. So I will choose faith over flesh fear y'all. As hard as it is ladies we must not lean on our own understanding. Anything is possible with God. I've surrendered my life, my addictions, my shortcomings, my daughter and families lives to him alone. Trusting the process is so hard because I literally have no flesh suit, sparrow, counselor, anyone with answers that we can talk to in here. It's all God's will for my life. To be quiet, be patient, be faithful and stand strong and brave. Then when something miraculous happens all the glory can be to God alone. That will be apparent even to the not so smart flesh because I've not been able to do or say anything or talk to any flesh that even has answers on my paperwork. Seems like God's angels have swooped down from heaven and they now have all my paperwork, sentence and will for my life. It's all in God's hands now. No wait ladies, it's always been in God's hands. I'm tired of worrying about the flesh suits, flesh sentences, flesh judgment. I'm so grateful, thankful God's now in full 100% control in my head. I will not fail I will not stumble I will not sink. Girls let's keep our eyes on the Holy Spirit heart hugs, eyes on the words of the bible and eyes and ears and hearts on God. Our father. He is the only way. Pray now pray hard pray throughout your stay. I love you God the savior of my life.

Gift of the word

YALL, MY RECOVERY BIBLE HAS BEEN SUCH A WONDERFUL AMAZING GIFT that I received here from this flock. That is probably the only thing positive I could say about this place. The recovery Bible then the rack up box sits with no speaking for hours at a time to be able to dig deep in that thing to gain the wisdom and knowledge that God wrote and spoke about through his word. That thing is saving my life before the real rescue. Pre save. We had another fire drill today during Bible study and I took it as a heart hug. Not only was there a big red fire truck but over four cars in a row that proceeded to drive by as the big fire truck was pulling in and you guessed it they were all red. Y'all I don't know what the red means yet but I keep hearing and my thoughts and underlining scriptures that the rescue is in red. Maybe it's because my car at home is red, who knows but God. So I'm just going to continue to read my recovery Bible spread the good news when I can to whoever will listen and continually surrender my heart and life to God. I've been inclined to surrender all my fears and anxieties of my daughter's life and my mom and families to the Lord. Y'all it gives you peace in your heart. I haven't been writing due to the reading of my Bible but y'all I have the world's worst cycles as a female and I had a migraine the other day so bad I almost started crying it hurt so much. I was scared to even ask for Tylenol or Advil but one of my flock mates asked the monitor on my behalf. Her name is a we will call A, she's very knowledgeable and sweet and has been to this flock before. She relapsed and ended up turning herself in again and we have become flock friends. She feels like home or has that mom like sense of comfort. She keeps telling me it's going to be OK and comforting me about my daughter. Like she said why would God not answer my prayers of goodness to protect my family. It's telling me over and over in the Bible that God's will and plans for me and my daughters and our children's life are good as long as we believe. I faithfully do and will never stop y'all. I think by now on this page of my journey y'all as the readers know my deep love for God, my father and I'm trusting my life and my families to him. He is our rock. Our refuge. Our healer. Our protector. Our savior. He will save you and me he will protect and rescue us he is listening.

Healed

ALCOHOL WAS MY DOC YALL I WROTE ABOUT THIS PREVIOUSLY AND SINCE I I have even presented an essay to my fellow flock mates about saying goodbye to the poisonous disease driven, death lurking and devil knocking substance. I hate it. I was not good when the drink was in or anywhere near my cup or on my lips. My daughter had to be a witness of this many times and I am incredibly remorseful and sorry to her. She doesn't even know how it affected her yet. God I'm taking personal inventory of all my bullhonkey that filled up my cup and I'm throwing that cup in the dump. God has literally taken the taste, the disease out and off of my lips. It's like a reborn awakening beyond any words y'all. I don't even like smelling hand sanitizer because I can smell alcohol. It makes me nauseous and gag and feel a sense of spoiled rotten or like eating glass. God can do that for whomever asks y'all. I never want that substance anywhere near myself or my home. I pray God is protecting my daughter from such things. I put her through enough with that bad habit addiction and allowing other human flesh suits to consume the substance around her as well. I pray God gives her the wisdom and knowledge he has shown so clearly to myself as I've sat here for 40 days plus the 23 in pre flock. That's a total of 63 days to read my God's words and pray and ask for forgiveness for letting that devil's beverage do so much negative in my life, my daughters and Mrs.F, the poor innocent mother like myself that incredibly tragic evening on January 12th 2021. God thank you for taking that addiction, habit, disease off my lips tongue and out of my hands and thoughts for eternity. I believe God can and will heal your addictions if you believe and ask and beg. I will no longer or ever be triggered or failed due to my everlasting love of my savior God my ABBA, father of my life. I know I am chosen as a willing vessel of God's power to spread what has happened to me. Only by God was I saved, healed and protected from what could have happened with the devil's cup. God took the whole disease off me cleared my memories, thoughts and partaking of that devil's substance. I praise you Lord for you're healing me from that disease and I know he can do the same for you ladies.

God's promises

....

ASK AND YOU SHALL RECEIVE, GOD DOESN'T BREAK HIS PROMISES TO US. I didn't receive an actual letter from my daughter or family but I did receive more envelopes that i could actually use. Yay y'all I already wrote my letters to my kiddo and my mom and gave them to the monitor to put in the mailbox for outgoing delivery tomorrow morning. I was so excited that was a God heart hug promise received covenant moment. Not only am I confessing my horrible sin today but yet again to y'all the readers, I prayed about it and my situation all day ladies. Then after 40 days I finally got more usable envelopes. Prayers abundantly answered. My family is alive. Unfortunately they sent yet another mini radio that didn't work out for me but I don't even care yet again. Seeing those pre printed cardinal bird envelopes was amazing. Faith over fear is a healer. God does answer our prayers not when or how we can even imagine. The red cardinal on the envelopes is a significant sign from our God another heart hug on a Tuesday. It's strange how even when I'm writing these pages for y'all and the letters I wrote home I am having whole conversations with y'all. I feel like someone is on the other end of the these pages like a phone call. I think I may need to be checked out. Just kidding but seriously I converse with my father God all day long. Then when pen meets paper, I am writing this as I'm pretending to be conversing with you the reader. Maybe we are in a coffee shop, dorm, jail, hospital or at home in your white comfy bedroom. In any case I'm praying this testimony and my tiny answered prayers from this recovery, rehab, jail, rejuvenation disastercation, final flock encourage you to ask God for help. Put your guard down for Jesus. Let him fill up your spiritual cup instead of the devil's cup. Check out of sinful realities and check into the word of God. I've been reading the word and highlighting scriptures so much that the promises and love god has are flying up from my Bible and smacking me right into my heart and soul y'all. It is the only comfort. His ways are the only ways. Be obedient to gaining the knowledge and his will for your life and that's when he answers your cries, prayers and panic outburst. This is something I'm constantly having to remind myself y'all know this because you're experiencing it with me as I share it. Look at each time I start to get derailed from my God, spirit train tracks, and I put my nose into the Bible and God's word, I pray and express my sorrows and needs and praises to God then bam he shows up far before I sink. It's only when I take my eyes off his words and will for my life and I'm not reading the words he distinctively put here for us to embrace, empower, embody drink up into our soul that I crack open the train and feel a slight drift of deviled derailing air tried to block or throw off course my whole life. Seriously ladies it's so important to focus on God. No matter how strong the force of Satan is God's power and love is so much more than anything we can ever imagine. This is my testimony true and directed and controlled by God only. Nothing I wrote is made-up or untrue. I write as God my father directs my path. This is for y'all and well myself to go back and encourage and empower myself and you. The reader. God thank you for allowing me to receive envelopes to write home and it gave me a sense of peace and faith and trust in my Lord all over again. Thank you for all you do for us and please continue to protect our families that we may not be at home with, those whom we have lost and those whom we have yet to meet. I trust your word and will for my life dear Lord. I love you. Ladies I'm going to pray for all of us and put the pen down and read my father's words till it's time to shut my eyes on yet another day the Lord has given us. Goodnight ladies, pray for everyone you love.

Distractions

. . . .

As I just set my Bible down and looked up to the TV the game plan is on and I saw that the main character is #1 like me here in my final flock bunk one. And his team is the color Crimson red he also just won the championship. I'm not sure whether this was a heart hug but I decided to record it for y'all just in case something amazing happens. Now they put on the letters to God, now this is more of a movie I will actually watch and enjoy. Y'all, I have become so infatuated, consumed, mesmerized and in complete awe of my God my father. He is always there right when I need him. Even when I don't know I need him. I love God so incredibly much it's an overwhelming satisfaction when we display his name, his power, and his glory in the place I'm currently in. Since I'm almost chief here at this dorm, I feel my calling and purpose is to ensure the Lord's name is constantly on my lips, my heart and my thoughts. Ladies fall in love with God become intimate in the Holy Spirit. It helps wherever you're at in your life journey be OK. Be at peace. His will for our lives is to fall in love with him embrace him through his word. Then we are to express our thankfulness and love and praise out loud in his name. This movie is a heart hug from God because it's about receiving mail. Letters from God. I can't wait to watch it and feel all the heart hugging emotions I know it will give. Just because as you all know I still haven't received mail from my flesh family. But the love mail, God mail, Jesus Holy Spirit mail heart hugs I've been receiving are abundant and amazing. So Lord please don't stop with the heart hugs letters from God. They are crucial for my and our survival here on this earth. Again, ladies we can't always change our situations but what we can do is change how we think about them, put God in our thoughts in situations and they don't seem to be so detrimental. They may still really bad but when we focus on God and all the great things God has done for us through us and towards our flesh families, we can somewhat feel content with whatever is going on. Pray through it, pray really hard and God will get us through the quicksand of doubt, fear and life. Be calm be still and remain patient. I know it's hard ladies trust me just because I'm writing these words of encouragement and empowerment I have to reread and consume them for myself because I don't always feel so chipper. Especially being trapped where I currently am. I miss my daughter and my mom and my family more than words could ever explain and I am trapped. I can't see, hear or haven't received mail from any flesh since I'm wearing a flesh suit my flesh heart hurts. But we must be brave and keep believing God's going to pull through for us just as he is and has done for all these people and situations I've been reading about in the Bible. God is good yesterday, today and tomorrow. He will not let us down if we place him and his word and Jesus holy spirit in the center of our universe. God Lord father is our only protector, encourager and savior. He is coming for our rescue ladies. God's timing is impeccable and not ours. So be quiet, wise and patient.

God's will

....

YALL, WE ARE JUST NOW ALLOWED TO FINISH LETTERS TO GOD AND THERE are so many heart hugs I'm receiving. Not only is it about like texting your best friend God through mailing letters to God but there was a scene with pippi longstocking and during our peer group game earlier that was the fictional character I chose that started with the letter P. Then they were bobbing for red apples. The conversation the mom had with her daughter whose name is Maddie that's my daughter's name was everything my mom tells me. I love this movie y'all so far I've teared up laughed multiple times. I love how much faith this little boy named Tyler has. Him and his best friend are so profound. It makes me miss my daughter and family but it's also making me comforted that God is in this place with me and I'm holding on to the rescue. I have to! I believe just as the movie is portraying and making me feel God's not done with us or me. I am here right where I am for a reason. Then the mail man's character is drinking alcohol a lot and just throws the bottle of alcohol because all his life he said anyone he touches turns to dust. He came into this little boy's life who has cancer, that's Tyler and things are going according to God's will for everyone. It's showing each character's path and plan that God has and how it lines up in certain situations places and introduced to certain people all through the will of God. God's timing is impeccable. We have to continually keep hope alive and have faith in our savior. Some of the places we are and have been may not feel very holy or even safe. But this little boy tyler knows when he dies of his cancer he was a chosen one from God to help someone else who's going through the same thing. How wonderful is it when our children can be stronger in their faith and hope than us as adults. We get stuck looking too far ahead and sometimes back to even learn the ultimate lessons. That's why God places us, stubborn learners in a solitary confinement, jail, devilcation, hospital or alone with our thoughts and our God and our bibles. So we can dig deep in our faith hope and love buckets. He won't leave us or forsake us. He may be testing us but it won't be for a long period. As long as we gain the wisdom say our prayers and follow our paths and direct instructions from the Bible, from god's word and laws we will be freed. Saved. My recovery bible is so highlighted it lights up my treasure box when I set it in there. It states over and over that he will rescue us. You, me, your families everyone. It says he will never leave you or forsake you. It says he loves you no matter what you have done. It says he reigns from heaven. It says you are forgiven. Then it says share this awakening, this love you found, this wisdom you have gained with the world. With your children. So do it ladies document your life for Jesus. It's only going to lead to a successful recovery and lifelong eternal love. He's waiting for us.

Patience in the waiting

BEING PATIENT IN THE WAITING IS BECOMING HARDER AND HARDER WHEN I'm still waiting and praying for a letter from my daughter. I reread the letter she wrote me a couple weeks ago, 4 to be exact but it just isn't the same without hearing her sweet voice and knowing she's safe and taken care of. I've had to control the panic feelings I constantly get when the devil overrides the holy spirit in my mind. God, please send me a heart hug or a sign of any sort to confirm my baby girl is OK. She's being fed and taken care of her new braces and holding the Fort down while I've been gone. I pray for protection over her and my mom. Y'all this is incredibly hard to redirect in my head. God send me your strongest most comforting heart hugs please please please. Also send my daughter heart hugs and comfort about the finances and allow her to be able to maintain the home while I'm gone. Yall my heart physically hurts again it's a pain you can't put into words. Like a deep knot in your throat and fire in your lungs. Fear and panic and disassociation. It's making me not be at peace here in this flock. Like something is really wrong at home. Girls we have to open the Bible and read the words of scripture because at this point I can't spiral out nor change anything about my current situation. I have to just try to change how I am thinking about it. One of my flock mates asked if I had bad motherly feeling like something was wrong and to be honest I don't know. I struggled to drown out the devil's whispers so they catch wind to my heart. I'm praying constantly that god is protecting her. Just makes me dislike the flesh sparrows and persecutors even more. There is no reason i shouldn't be able to make that phone call to settle my heart. I'm a single parent and did my daughter's only constant for her whole almost 17 years of existence. I swear it feels like a neglect and absence of dignity in here. Not to even allow me to send a letter in an envelope I have in my property. Y'all the system is broken. What we can count on is the heart hugs from our father our god. I'm praying hard today for a tiny speck of light to be spread on this dark cloudy devil plan and thoughts. God take away the devil's words oppression accusations and fear. I'm holding on to the good news of the

Lord. Y'all, I haven't even been writing in my book for y'all because I've been as I said disassociated and pulled out and away from my Holy Spirit vibes by a strong force from the devil. Ladies, please pray with me and for me and your families in times of devil trials. He really does come to kill still and destroy. If you're locked up get locked into your bible and those silent moments with no family communication. God will and is protecting them and when he's ready to ease your fears and panic he will. He's making a way and building endurance and character not only in us but our families and our friends. Pray, pray, pray! And then pray some more. Have faith, be graceful and thankful that we are alive and trust that God's working in every aspect of our lives. Yes, he is ladies. God is our rock, our foundation. The truth, the way and the life. In his name we pray thank you Jesus son of God for protecting us and our children and families while we work on ourselves and our assignments for the Lord. Amen.

Let go and let God

....

ANOTHER MIDWEEK DAY HERE IN MY FINAL FLOCK, FLOCK MATES AND ladies. I have one word for this whole thing and it's chaos absolute devil chaos. We are already overcrowded with 32 ladies and we just got word that there are 9 more waiting a couple doors down the hall, an intake where it all begins. Y'all we already sit on these treasure boxes for hours at a time due to the overcrowding. On a more positive note, I got the red heart hug of the century this morning while walking back from chow hall. A little red heart hug I got was the strawberry on the cream cheese they gave for our bagels. But the big finale one was the incredible red sky sunrise y'all. No joke I've never seen the sky this color. The sun was slowly waking up and making her appearance far to the left of where we were walking, and it was painting the sky in the most magnificent bright red. That was a heart hug from God y'all. No doubt. Earlier this morning as I was chatting with my father at 4:00 AM. I just kept feeling at peace to surrender my whole life once again to the Lord. God, please protect my daughter and family and myself and my flock mates and their families at home. Guide me through the yucky mud and waterless dungeon I'm currently residing in. I was reading a new book yesterday called God's will for you by Gloria Copeland and y'all those thoughts of fear, depression and anxiety are Satan! Although I know this, I love, love, love, getting reminders and heart hugs to know and confirm that those negative things are Satan and God is still working on my release, my life and my sentence. He reigns from heaven y'all. His will and plans for my life for your life are those of good and eternal life. We will be rescued ladies. I pray that with tears in my eyes as I gazed at the red sunrise. Then I was content in the closing of my prayer in Jesus name. I know God is and has been protecting and guiding my daughter as well.

Y'all as women we tend to have the urge and calling to control things. The household, bills, children and animals. But we need to let go and let God. I've had to continually say this lately let go and let God. God, I trust you and I love you, my daughter, your daughter our families are being protected and watched over by our father God and the Holy Spirit,

Jesus Christ. Continually surrender all our anxieties, fears and worries to him. I hadn't had a red heart hug that significant in a hot moment if you all remember it was a couple pages previously. For me the time between pages and heart hugs are days and weeks, for the reader it will be minutes and pages. I can't wait to proofread all this I've been blessed to portray on behalf of my Lord and savior and feel it as it will end. With my rescue from the flock by my Lord and savior. God Jesus the Holy Spirit please hear my cries. Cries of gratitude, praise and a little sadness from the absence of my daughters and family's life. Hear me O heavenly father. I'm knocking, I'm seeking, I'm asking and begging for you to come find me here in this final flock and save me. You saved and won my heart please rescue my flesh. Rescue my flesh and free me from this flock. I won't stop, my lord my father until his will is done for me in his name. I trust you lord I'm letting go and letting God every day until I am rescued. Ladies continually do the same.. there is no other name but the name of Jesus!

Back on the magic school bus

I'M SITTING HERE THINKING OF ALL THE WAYS I CAN MAKE OATMEAL AT home. Cut up bananas in there, strawberries, blueberries or well y'all all the fruits. I can't wait to prepare a meal for my flesh family. I hope whatever meal you had today left you satisfied and not overstuffed. I thanked Jesus all the way to the table we sat out for the day the birds chirping and the breath in my lungs. I also prayed for the sparrow guards, one isn't in too good of shape and she can barely walk. Even though she respectfully called me out she didn't say my name which I just wanted to thank her for. So, I am the one who got in my treasure box at 4:48 AM to grab a toothbrush and toothpaste. Y'all that's a big no no whenever the lights are off here. Good Lord have mercy on whoever created these flock rules. Seriously I'm praying for them because I know for 100% fact no one that is working here has been through the program like a real flock mate. Honestly a lot of them would never win at their own game. I'm certain this flock is broken but ladies let's get back to some heart hug positivity Philippians 4:5 let everyone see that you are considerate in all that you do. 6 don't worry about anything instead pray about everything tell God what you need and thank him for all that he has done. 7 then you will experience God's peace which exceeds anything That we can understand. The commercial 444 444 just came on heart hug. His peace will guard your hearts and minds as you live in Christ Jesus. #8 and now dear brothers and sisters one final thing fix your thoughts on what is true and honorable and right and pure and lovely and admirable. Think about the things that are excellent and worthy of praise. #9 keep putting into practice all you learned and received from me everything you heard from me and saw me doing. Then the God of peace will be with you. I had to write those words out of scripture because I keep seeing those buses drive by in my head. Like a heart hug that I am going to be the teacher, coach, encourager through Jesus Christ who saved me and equipped me with the proper armor tools and gear to do that y'all. When scriptures and the words from the Bible precisely line up with the words, I have been obedient to relay on this paper for y'all that's Jesus. Jesus. Jesus.

Jesus, you make the darkness tremble. Y'all I missed that song. It was one of my daughter my favorite songs called Tremble. You silence fear Jesus Jesus you make the darkness tremble Jesus Jesus. Go listen to that song now if you can and think of, paint a picture in your mind of what that would look like. I just got the opposite of what felt like a heart pain. It's been a weird day of cleaning and showering and no outside time the TV has been on pretty much all day. I've been proofreading this book for y'all and myself to make sure I didn't sound boring which this testimony is anything but boring y'all. I'm incredibly proud of myself and I'm only on page what I thought was 54 probably because I keep getting pulled away for unnecessary reasons. Back to the heart pain I had to pause and write about finally we were called to see the property man and to see if we had anything sent from our loved ones. He was bald and spunky and kind, but he grabbed my drop paper and said do you live out of town because this paper has a phone number that doesn't seem like it's in the area that just means I've been here for this long and again none of my family has been called. What the flock. I cried when I sat back on my box to write this because it felt like my flesh family forgot about me but now as I'm finishing writing about it, I don't need anything from home anyway. I keep holding back tears with a huge lump in my throat saying in my head that I'm OK. Jesus hasn't forgot about me. He hasn't forgot about you ladies either. I have clothes, shoes, food and water. And most importantly this pen the notebook to share the heart pain. So heart pain turned to heart hug. It still hurts my little feelers. Again, as I wrote the date 4/18 it was my pre flock bunk number. Heart hug again just a reminder that I am OK from the Holy Spirit. I'm taking a deep breath ladies and wiping my tears so I can go back to proofreading. Butterfly kisses y'all we were walking back from chow I was taking in the fresh air and listening to the cute birds chirping. Then I made a comment about how pretty the white butterflies are and y'all one literally flew by my cheek and the flock mate behind me said butterfly kisses. That was a heart hug like no other because there's a song your dad sings to his daughter about that, and the Lord is my father and he sent that white pretty butterfly kiss to me. I loved it and I teared up. During peer group and this CDC substance group I heard fighter jets flying over my flock. They are loud but I was just prompted to say they are reminders heart hugs that the army God prepares will find me. My rescue from this flock, air fighter jets. Now y'all I know I won't be rescued by a plane or a jet fighter fleshbots, but my rescue is coming. They have been flying over all day. Every time I hear them I smile and say in my head I will rescue you. He, Jesus will send out an army to find me in the middle of the darkest night is true, I will rescue you.

Obedience

DEUTERONOMY 11: 8 THEREFORE BE CAREFUL AND FOLLOW MY COMMAND I am giving you today, so you may have strength to go in and take over the land you are about to enter. #9 if you obey you will enjoy a long life in the land that the Lord swore to give to your ancestors and to you their descendants a land flowing with milk and honey. 10 for the land if you carefully obey the commands, I am giving you today and if you love the Lord your God and serve him with all your heart and soul, 14 then he will send the rains in the proper seasons the early and late rains. 16 but be careful do not let your heart be deceived so that you turn away from the Lord and serve and worship other gods. The Lord's anger will burn against you. Wow this testimony will go even a step further ladies it is in your hand, yours and now it has given you the strength and power to pass it along. I cannot express how honored I am to be able to be obedient to what the Lord has so gracefully given me to do this was a hard assignment, but I know it was meant to be read, seen and heard by you. My flock mates, my soul sisters, my flesh suits the sparrows. I prayed about what verses to share next and Deuteronomy was where the marker was wedged into. Heart hugs on the daily y'all. Can I get an Amen. Ohh and y'all I was just thinking about chow how I wanted some chocolate in our snack today was a nutty bar. Heart hug. Thank you Lord my father for all the blessings you gave today allowed me to share with my soul sisters, the readers and flock mates. I will say my hand is rather tired from writing, so I will take a pen break for the evening unless Im moved to share again. Deuteronomy is such a great reference or story to read before you lay your head down ladies.

Smiling is my favorite

SMILING IS MY FAVORITE IN MY FLOCK I HOPE YOU WHOEVER WHEREVER you have been able to get your hands on this book and are enjoying it. I want nothing more in my life to make even one person smile a day. So, smile now show those chompers. If you don't have any like how they did not let grandma have hers ladies. No judgments that is why they made mashed potatoes and blenders for that matter. You are wonderfully made, beautiful and bold. Claim it today claim it every day. The next couple scriptures are great too because it's saying find a place of worship, he himself will I know for a fact hillside fellowship is my Church of choice in spring branch TX. I cannot wait to go introduce myself to the pastor and be bold and brave and get connected more than I ever have before. I want to share this whole testimony and hear yours. Spread the good news like wildflowers. Outside they cut the grass the other day and of course all the flowers and the next day those little boogers were already sprouted back up. Even the white ones in the same path. Y'all these are heart hugs I do not forget to look at daily.

Bible school

So, I did that thing where you say a prayer and look up, Lord whatever you want me to read right now let me open it to the page. And drum roll proverbs 2 and well through three I'm going to read it more and then once I wait for the direction from my father to speak on it. I keep trying to plan out how I'm going to type this testimony, then recorded as well with my voice full effects of my personality. I need to find out how to publish a book. I can't Google it in here laugh out loud the Bible is my Google, but technology has slightly expanded from the time the Bible was written. I know the Lord will put the right flesh suits together to help me get this thing out but I will say it's kind of exciting thinking about sitting up in the early morning at home with a nice warm cup of coffee and typing this out for you my readers and my soul sisters. I can't wait to wake up before my daughter while she's sleeping in her bed and I could see her tucked in And be looking out the window comfy in my white room then the sun beaming through my windows with rainbows all around. Lord God my father I'm ready to type I'll send those prayers up as I lay my head down in my flock. What a nice thing to look forward to right y'all. I'm going to pray for my rescue warriors to hurry up father God I love you and I trust you when I do get a hold of my laptop to type in Minnie and penny will follow me around and try to sit on my workload. I will know that is the ultimate heart Hug. in Jesus name I pray this evening amen. I pray I dream about what I just imagined asking you shall receive seeking you shall find knock and the door will be open.

Wake up call and against my Will they are making me wear shorts. I don't wanna wear shorts. I never wear shorts. I'm sad this morning. The flesh suit sparrows really are not OK and I am praying for them. It's been 11 months., almost a whole year since I've shown my legs in public y'all I don't know why, but this was going to make me cry. I don't wanna be here in this place wearing these ugly boy shorts and the sparrow guards aren't even wearing shorts. Wow I didn't know how this was going to affect me. No one should make you have to show your legs if you don't want to.

I'm violated today Against my own free Will. There's a lot of rules and regulations and y'all I follow them all. But putting on a pair of ugly long shorts, shouldn't be a control. The flesh has over me or you. I keep trying to hide my tears, but I'm shaking and can't. I'm talking to one of the guard sparrows and she tried to vouch for me, but then we got into a deeper Convo about how her sparrow boss treats her. She's discriminated against in her position as a monitor because she has compassion and empathy, which are great human traits. She gave out books to some of the residents. We are flock mates and got called on her personal time off at home. She's also not as quick when walking due to some disabilities, but she's been here for eight years and they will only let her work the night shift. Y'all she's the sweetest cutest grandma style sparrow guard. I told her I'm praying for her. She then began to tell me she's again been here for eight years and at 10 they give some kind of something job security. I don't know then I told her she is doing exactly what they are doing to us. Counting the days and following the unnecessary roles to get those 10 years. I'm all about structure and roles but not OK with breaking hearts, crushing spirits. I view the monitors as one with me because we are all God's children. Not one flesh suit in this place is better or more worthy of anything. We are all equal here, ladies. Don't let the devil's word fool you. Don't worship a false idols. These flush suits are temporarily in control of your flesh suit, just your physical outer body. Not your heart, your mind or your spirit. Let's send prayers out now to those who have persecuted us, falsely accused, discriminated, violated, abuse, and emotionally tried to scar us. God says no. He won't allow his children, his daughters to have to endure such pain at persecution. I know I said pain and tears may come in the night, but joy comes in the morning, but then neglect dishonor misjudgments can happen at 5 AM. They can happen at any time of the day. The good news is Joy will still come. You have a father, God, Jesus Christ, and the Holy Spirit that will come to your rescue. It won't matter where you are if it's night or day. If it's storming or sunny if you are a monitor or higher if you're in red blue purple, green or rainbow. He is coming to rescue you us, me. In those moments of weakness, just pray and cry it out. Who cares who judges you on the way of wearing the shorts the why of why you don't want to be looked at or seen naked. This world is so full of bullies, It's beyond hard. Heart Hugs after the shorts thing happened when I was talking to the precious grandma monitor we will call her. She is also interested in my book. She probably didn't even pick up on what she labeled me but when we were talking about her time here the eight years and the number of days and reasons for the colored shirts. I told her I wanted a rainbow shirt which she smiled, but then I said the Lord my father is the only one who can number your days and your position here. She disregarded and said well you have plenty of time in here to write so your book will be interesting. Grandma I'm going to pray for you and for your pain release on your legs and back. And for the other monitors to not bully. Whatever you have going on at home, don't you dare try to label, color code or number my days here. That was the devil's puppet talking. I'm different not better not worse not colored I'm a child of the highest Lord god my father. The holy spirit is in me and for me so who can be against me or you.I wanted so badly to stand up for myself this morning but I didn't. I prayed for my father to heart hug me. He did by easing my fears and anxieties. No one should have to feel that way. If you have or you do at this moment of reading this I'm heart hugging you and look up at whatever is in your view whether it be dirty ceiling a cloudy sky, a mirror, a wall, blue sky or bars and you pray my soul sister. Ask God to comfort your heart. Rescue you, brave you, change you, heal you, protect you, love you. Our father who art in heaven hallowed be thy name thy kingdom come thy will be done on earth as it is in heaven.

Heart hug cues

So, I'm minding my own little Natalie business deep into writing scriptures for you all to reference and y'all I have good ears. The monitor standing next to me and my bunk were talking about their daughters and TikTok. Heart hug that my mommy epiphanies and heart hugs are now confirmed. They continued on and said y'all what did it used to be before TikTok and I said musically. That's what my daughter started out doing then I smiled from heart to cheek. That conversation in front of me and my ears happened for a reason. God the Holy Spirit want me to hear that heart hug y'all. Are you listening for heart hugs and cues. It took me being away from the crowd who's all watching TV and playing cards deep into my Bible to hear that. Glad I didn't miss it I needed that confirmation. The Bible study leader has a soft voice with white pants and beautiful presents. We listened to Newsboys Christ alone be converted she's speaking about a woman who was in Bexar county and she works there now. Recovery coach, that's what I want to do y'all. She's so cute and says she needs to walk every morning. I can't wait to get out of here y'all and walk. She also said that rejection is God's protection. I took notes in the middle of my thoughts to y'all but it ended up working out perfectly in Jesus name. The Bible study was confirmation that this book will help whoever's hands and eyes and ears it grazes upon. The group leader was the perfect Jesus warrior she's a single parent she gets up early to walk and that's just like me y'all in the free. I think that's why this flock is making me digress or feel like I'm digressing. I can't maintain my healthy lifestyle and the Jesus habits I was already forming with my family flock. I can't wait to take again I think I've written this whole sentence my red car piled with my daughter and my mom and family and drive down to 281 northbound to spring branch where I will attend hillside fellowship on Sundays. How I long for those days. God will take this moment to thank you for sending the Holy Spirit warriors to speak to us today along with the heart hugs and confirmed and shared in there as well. I love you and I trust you and I pray you go into the reader's heart and place of worship as well. Wherever that may be. Be converted into a Christ like life. Believe in him alone peace will be with you and in you and thanks miss frizzle, devil puppet counselor for all my Jesus card ideas. I'll put them out on the daily y'all.

Squeeze and mop

Mapping that's the dorm chore Chapman was assigned to. I was excited y'all because I was kind of getting writers block again. Plus it gets me moving and I can squeeze my abs while I do it. Y'all the day room is the largest area to mop plus since I don't have community service hours to do they can put it towards any fees I owe for my stay here at the Holiday Inn. All jokes aside I thought of Yvonne and how she mopped with grace and pride. Heart hug so I will too do my chore with pride. Little do they know I'm working out when I do it squeeze and mop ladies. I thank God for the opportunity to do my part in mopping to please my father. Ladies you have to do all things for the Lord take pride in any chore, job, assignment he allows to fall across your path. Mopping for the Lord. I wasn't too bad at it either I've used a swiffer before but this is an old school mop and bucket. I prayed and mopped and tightened my abs now ladies I will go back to doing my scripture education and writing them down as I reference as well. Y'all know that's how I retain information by writing it. I have to see, write, say repeat. As I was sitting here still trying to get my thoughts together I see all these younger girls laughing and having fun in here. All I can think about is laughing with my family. Then I had to hold back tears because I need a hug a real hug heart hugs all the hugs. I'm having to repeat God I trust you and I love you and I know the plans you have for me are good. I still haven't talked to a flesh suit counselor one-on-one or my PO even though I put a request in. I'm assuming like when you go to the doctor no news is good news. I am praying that a letter I wrote to the judge that my daughter received the day before my flock move got to the correct flesh suit, who would read and pray about my situation. I pray they spoke to the Lord my father ended his will and way. I pray Maddie got my letter the apology with the skittle rainbow spit the one that I mailed from my final flock reminding her to pray me out. Ensuring she's fighting for me prayers do work ladies. I also hope she received it so she can dig deep into her Bible and educate herself while I'm away. Find peace with the Lord while I'm at this place. I really want to hold on to the heart hugs I've been given so far and asked for more, but I don't want to be selfish with God's time. Lord I'm thanking you for everything you have given to me thus far. Your name is forever imprinted on my heart soul and lips I can't wait to share my knowledge with Maddie and the world as God allows it.

Heart guard

HAPPY SUNDAY Y'ALL OR WHATEVER DAY OF THE WEEK IT IS THAT YOU'RE finding yourself indulged in this book. We woke up to a sergeant sparrow today which on Sunday ladies, really is it necessary? That means this woman woke up and she's determined to crush some spirits and bully. There will definitely be some write ups today which is sad because this is Sunday the Sabbath day a great day to be alive. She also already put it on my heart that we would be doing indoor recreation, TV time and no body movement y'all. I am so glad I woke up at 6:00 AM and already had my motivation conversations with the Lord my father from bunk number one. Once I get back in and situated from chow and oppression I will share my deep beautiful heart hug conversations. Remember ladies, the sparrows and devil puppet sergeants can use their words and power to try and crush you but just pray. Pray your anxieties, fears, shortcomings, oppressions and stones thrown away. God won't let them get into your heart. He is the best heart guard. Sparrow devil puppet is on a mission for write ups confirmed all the dos and don'ts we heard on our journey across the catwalk were minute and undeserving but ladies beware sometimes unfortunately these powerful devil puppets have flesh like weapons that they can use to demote, degrade, humiliate and discriminate with against you and your soul. Again, in these times when your flesh is being controlled listen, shut your mouth and do as you are told but pray the whole way through it. They can't take your Jesus time.

Devil Dream robbed

THIS BRINGS ME TO TOO MUCH SLEEP IS THE DEVIL SLEEP. I WAS JUST reading about this in scripture either yesterday or the day before and it actually happened to me. Ladies 8 hours is all we need my body fortunately usually wakes me up from my hummingbird heart after six or seven. So, the first 8:00 AM wake up I woke up four hours ahead at 4:20 if you remember. I had no bad dreams and it wasn't restless. It was perfect and sound like a baby I'm assuming. Then last night which was Saturday I went to sleep at 9:00 PM. I woke up at 2:00 PM around 4:00-ish and made myself fall back to sleep, nope. I had horrible dreams from 4:00 to 6:00 AM. That was when the devil was allowed to come in and rob my peace y'all. Getting too much sleep isn't good, it's restless, it's the gateway for the devil to creep into your mind your thoughts and your dreams. The holy spirit put me directly by the clock for a reason so that I could record this in the raw for you. That's why I checked the time to record the events in my mind and come to pen to paper with them when movement is allowed. Ladies wake up earlier use that time before the world around you wakes up to have coffee with your father. Walk with your father, whatever it is get out of the flipping bed. If you can't like me at the moment, talk to God he will get your mind right for the day. Pray, converse and convert. Plus, y'all in my other flock I learned all the body squeezes from my bed remember. Ladies, this was a good conversation with the Lord our father. So, as I'm lying there doing my left bottom squeezes then my right, then all together now. A light bulb in my head, mind and heart went on. Glory be to God. I wrote about how God my father our father is the only control system of our lives. I've reiterated this numerous times because it's the truth, the way and the life. No sparrow, no judge, no lawyer, no devil puppet, no devil sergeant, no flesh suit on earth has authority over what God has already planned for you, me, your sisters, your brothers and anyone from another mother. God the Lord is our only judge he has the mallet, the paperwork, the control center to our souls. In scripture it even says he will rescue, you save, you free, you not because of anything you or I did. We can't be good girls make all A's never talk back to get what God's planned. He is going to do it regardless. He sets prisoners free y'all from the deep waters. The Lord gets all the glory and all the praise when he rescues us. We are stubborn people, but he will come and save you from oppression ladies. So it was put on my heart to say I haven't spoken to the PO the counselor or the judge and it wouldn't matter what the letter they got if they wanted to release me or if they wanted to contain me. God's plan is not theirs. Y'all so when your rescue happens when you're removed by the Holy Spirit when you're not judged because the Lord is for you and when you just believe he comes to your rescue it won't be because of anything you did or didn't do. It won't be because of any flesh suit talked to this flesh suit and made a plan, filled out the paperwork. It will be because your father loves you ladies. It won't even be because you followed or didn't follow all the rules or if you're in blue, yellow, green or black. All the glory be to God. So, ladies when it happens proclaim it give it all the likes streaks glory fame applause to God. Glorify his name alone. Spread his good news we are stubborn people that the Lord forgave if you believe and ask him daily to come into your heart. Like I have and will continue and when my rescue comes it won't be anything but the glory to my father. I told you the morning flock talks with my father can bring me to tears. I cried a lot this morning, peace be with you tears. From the Bible study yesterday to every single heart hug minute. I've thanked my father for the air in my lungs the food which I have received and about to receive. The strength in my wrist and fingers to write, the patience and wisdom and knowledge to be able to write and transform my prayers and thoughts into words I can share with y'all the reader. I was laying in bed at 8:30 PM last night finishing up my schedule writing and the last words that were put on me to share through this book and had the sudden urge heart hug to read some of my work. I ended up starting on the part where I would be typing up this testimony with my family and cats and as silly as it may seem I read to the last pages, and it gave me the exact peace I needed before I shut my eyes y'all. I'm ecstatic to know that even though I'm writing this when I went back to check it out for myself it helped me be at peace and fall asleep like a baby. No fears just confirmation to know that my father was with me, still and I got heart hugs all over again. Ladies, I truly hope, pray and believe this book will do something to your heartstrings as well. I pray with the words I've chosen to relay from the Holy Spirit glide across your eyes, ears and you can form your own visions and imagery that connects it to your life with your situation. Your flock life. Your home life.

Surrender novena

Y'ALL I JUST GOT DONE WITH MY DAILY SHOWER AFTER INDOOR recreation which y'all I don't know when you jumped rope the last time but that is a skill. Not only physically but mentally on when to jump as soon as the rope gets to your feet. It was kind of like how they say it's like riding a bike. Something you just don't forget, then I was moved to say to myself like prayer should be just a constant good reminder. In your head every day. Then I sat on my box and read the surrender novena from Pam's Bible study yesterday. And here is what it says Ladies, Day 2 surrender to me does not mean to fret to be upset or to lose hope nor does it mean offering to me a worried prayer asking me to follow you and change your worry into prayer. It is against the surrender deeply against it to worry to be nervous and to desire think about the consequences of anything. It is like the confusion that children feel when they ask their mother to see to their needs and then they try to take care of those needs for themselves so that childlike efforts get in their mother's way. Surrender means to place close the eyes of the soul to turn away from the thoughts of tribulation and to put yourself in my care so that only I act saying you take care of it. Heart hug, I've been overthinking about well everything after I write it and I deeply needed to read that and surrender my flesh thoughts and say Jesus I surrender the problems the worry and the time to you. Then ladies it has a little mantra you can say to yourself out loud or to your brain: ohh Jesus I surrender myself to you take care of everything. So take the time to say this more than 10. I'm going to sing it to myself all the way to chow, down the catwalk in my beautiful red shirt and oversized blue crocs and bushy eyebrows ladies. Isn't that lovely to come back and read after this flock served corn dogs at chow. Yuck I am not and have never been a fan of corn dogs. Funny heart hug though, I've realized that at every meal there is something on my plate Madi would love. Like the corn dog, the bread pudding, the mashed potatoes, yep that's a heart hug. I'm glad I'm aware of the small things y'all should to look around wherever you are and take in those little things. The food your daughter would enjoy, those tiny white flowers in a field of yellow ones, a single white rose in a bushel, the crisp air blowing in your lungs, the birds chirping and grabbing worms from the moist soil. Those are the heart hugs from God.

You do not got mail

LADIES I'M SITTING ON MY BUNK AT MY STAYCATION AND I GRABBED A book yesterday called The Invitation", by Sarah Bush. We just got back from chow and I was moved to read her book instead of watching tv, which is currently on and far too loud. But as I am reading the chapter called the covenant promises not only is the scripture from Genesis 9:12-16 which is about rainbows but her personal journal entries on her quotes, heart hugs, that she calls signs that the Lord God is with her and her kids when she sees a rainbow in any form. Then as I continue reading she's speaking about the Lord's miraculous signs of power, protection and presents showing his love to the Israelites. He even parted the Red Sea y'all, he led them through their journey with a cloud by day and a fire by night. This heart hugged me. I kept thinking about my red heart hugs and how and when I've I've had them the fire alarm during group, the red exit sign, the red folder holding paperwork. All the red cars that just happened to go by while I'm paying attention. I still believe now today on this day April 27th 2024 Saturday at 2:35 PM God is here with me and red has something miraculous that will happen in the red. God my father thank you for these heart hugs. I now am settled at peace knowing you are working on my paperwork, and even if it's at night you'll have a fire guide me by its light, and my exit will be in red. If he can part the Red Sea y'all and walk on water there is no flesh that can keep me prisoner when God sets me free! Now I'm sitting in a Bible study and the cute little ladies have red nails and white and red converse shoes. Before I came to this flock Madi's dad had her memorize Psalm 23. They are talking about this in our bible study. The Lord is my shepherd, I shall not want. So many heart hugs and red today and through scripture. Even just now I am sitting on my bunk about to start reading more of Mrs. Bush's book and that song, I paint the town red came on the TV. Y'all the TV is so loud in here I mean I can't focus all the way. I dislike this very much. I still walk the catwalk to chow with my prayers going up to the lord for my rescue and my daughter and family to be safe. Every time the sparrows announced that there is mail my ears light up in the hopes I get something from my family. It's going on many days and I did mail a letter to my daughter and mom because they are basically close to the same place. Y'all we have to hold on to hope. Hope that the no news, no letter is good news. That's how it is for when you go to the doctor. When they see you, ladies we all know if they don't call back we are usually in the clear. Although this is incredibly different, I'm just patiently waiting to hear anything from my little Madi bug. I'm going to just pray they are working hard on getting me out or something amazing or maybe it's a long long letter. Who knows but y'all I get it, I know how sad, frustrating, lonely and secluded this can feel. But I look up to God and pray each time saying if God would send me a heart hug to confirm Madi is OK. There was cornbread on my plate I didn't eat, Madi would have eaten it though. She loves cornbread that was a heart hug. Heart hugged again with the same cornbread that I didn't eat but my daughter would. It's now been 37 plus days since I haven't spoken to my daughter or family. But I'm holding firm in faith that my God is protecting her and them. I'm continually surrendering our lives to God and my father. We have to hold on to faith y'all just believe.

Grace

....

IMMEDIATELY JESUS REACHED OUT HIS HAND AND CAUGHT HIM. YOU of little faith he said why did you doubt me Matthew 14; 25 through 31. This is a lot like how I've been praying and thinking lately. One minute I'm saying my father walks on water, the next I'm over here counting the days and listening to sparrows number and color code them. But even when Peter is told to come, seeing waves and letting his fear and doubt sink in, taking his eyes and focus off the one who sustains him, his miracle moment quickly became a moment of unbelief, how we as humans sometimes are. But not a second pass before the hand of grace was reaching out to catch him. Y'all that's a sign, covenant, promised to us as well, he's reaching his hand out for you and I as well. Not a second goes by even in our fear, doubt, unbelief is the Lord not working behind the scenes on our behalf ladies. Then we are handed pictures of Jesus in front of a judge in a court setting with shackles. Answering our prayers. Y'all as I'm writing this one of the sparrows is saying since this is a 4 by 6 picture we are not allowed to have it in our locker boxes. Are you flocking kidding me Satan. That is a different kind of heart hug. Take it away, I have already talked about it and painted a picture of it in my mind. But y'all that just goes to show you the beast sparrows are devil puppets, but little do they know speaking about the picture even if it was taken away doesn't stop it from spreading the good news. So have that devil woman. She even said she was going to talk to the Bible church ladies that passed them out. Y'all this place is evil or has evil in it. I need my father to hurry up before they drain the light and sparkle out of my heart and eyes. But even as Peter y'all he's still coming have faith, love and hope with grace in the wait. Then another diversion from the devil flush came right after my positive confirmations about my rescue. Mr. F just called me to see if I wanted to add anything to my drop like stuff I may need for a longer stay here at this disastercation. God, please come back and heart hug me and take away those Satan noises and things out of my thoughts. I told y'all ladies the devil comes to steal kill and destroy. Even try to interrupt your hope from your prayers and God's communication with you. Don't let it pray away the Sparrow negativity motives. I trust you Lord and I love you I have hope and faith my God is still coming sooner than later.

Letters to God

GODFATHER AND YOUR SON JESUS CHRIST HEAR MY PRAYER JESUS I KNOW you have heard my cries. I know I have sinned and that you have forgiven me because you died on the cross for our sins and my sins. So that I may have eternal life. I believe God the father sent you as a living sacrifice. I praise you day and night. I long for the Holy Spirit to be with me and in me from now and until eternity. I love you Lord father with all my heart and I will keep your commandments. I will teach my daughter and my family and the world about your good news. About you about your son Jesus Christ. I believe with my whole body and soul that you are here and you are with me. I'm asking pleading in your name Jesus Christ that you come and rescue me from this final flock. Free me from this place I am crying and pleading in your name. I trust you and I love you and there won't be a day that goes by that all the glory will be to you God alone and your son Jesus Christ. In your beloved name I pray Amen period.

Y'all I read this prayer or this letter to God over 30 times and I would record the day and time that I read it and each time I felt the presence of the Holy Spirit with me and in me. So write your prayers say your prayers and don't forget to pray today.

Specific prayers

Y'ALL SO I WOKE UP 10 MINUTES BEFORE OUR 5:00 AM WAKE UP BUT I spent the little time alone with my father even then. It's a Monday on this side of the book and the sparrows we have today and tomorrow babysitting our flock are like ninja sergeant's. Needless to say it's been an eventful day I've spent my walks to chow praying to God about my rescue and I even wrote a letter prior to Jesus, God and the father because y'all scripture told me, tells us to pray using the holy spirit's name, Jesus Christ our Lord and savior. So I wanted to document it because scripture was correct as always I hadn't said the prayer so intentional and purposeful previously. I sealed it with his name then y'all I'm getting ready for our peer group and Mr. F calls me out again. Remember he's the one who handles the drop items here at disastercation. Sure enough I was sent envelopes and a personal stereo but to both I could not use. Envelopes were stamped on not printed and the radio was something you plug into a cell phone. Ha I call holy moly bologna, but there is a more, a letter from my daughter. I don't even care about the radio, music will make me miss my family even more. My daughter wrote the most profound intellectual heartwarming hug letter I've ever received. Ladies she's a 16 year old girl who never looks away from her cell phone for more than a TikTok second. I cried my eyes out and I hadn't even read it yet. I loved seeing her handwriting and knowing she had touched these pages with her beautiful skin. Her hands gracefully glided along the pages as I had eyes filled with the most comforting proud brave tears I have ever cried before. She is OK, mom, me, Natalie I'm doing a pretty good job at raising her even when I'm absent. This goes to show us ladies we are the role models for our kids and generations to come. Keep praying for them even when you're apart, together or face to face. Pray with them. God hears our prayers and y'all that was a heart hug. Look back a couple pages, where I was patiently waiting for a letter, mail, heart hug and a sign that my daughter was OK. The letter I received by God's grace was the answer to my prayer. On his time y'all. He knows what we need when we need it. I was even thinking today before I got the letters that God not only answers my prayers, he answers yours, our daughters and our families. He reigns from heaven, and he works on our behalf even when we may feel forgotten, lost, not missed, unloved, unworthy, that's the flesh devil puppets distracting us from our father's love and plans. Keep praying, keep purposely praying and praising our god. Thank him wholeheartedly for answered prayers and especially when they are so clear and precisely answered. All the glory be to God! I got that picture of Jesus Christ in front of the judge just in time, I got my letters from home just in time, divine time. God's timing and holy spirit heart hugged me and more. Overflowing my grace and thankful cup for Jesus. Then ladies that's why we document these things because it shows how God is in control room of our lives and hearts. He is going to answer our prayers no matter how derailed the sparrows untracked our trains. Pray for those who persecute you lie to you and try to bring you down or make you believe anything other than what God says about you. Document the wrongfulness that way when the Lord does answer your prayers when God saves you, frees you from addiction, heart hugs you abundantly and frees you from a prison, speaks to the heart of a judge or a lawyer on your behalf. You had it documented. Sealed and approved by your God father and the Holy Spirit. Because that's how the good news gets viral, write it, send it, share it. Speak it, read it, write it, rewrite it, sing it all the praise be to God alone y'all. I am only able to write these pages by the grace, faith and love from Jesus Christ. I am only brave because he is here with me in this place. He's made it very apparent to you and me as I go back and read my Jesus card pages y'all, the scripture is always backed up by a heart hug or experience I'm documenting. This book is only being transformed into my testimony of my rescue because my father ordained it to be so. It's happening by his way. I'm reading, learning, listening and growing into who he has called me to be. I am to empower, encourage, love, share and testify my God is real. He is and always has been the author of my life. I'm going to make sure this book is not only in your hands, your brothers, your sisters, your moms, and your flock. All the flocks will have a copy.

Armor of protection

IT'S MEMORIAL DAY WEEKEND, SATURDAY MAY 25TH 2024 ON MY END OF the pages y'all. Celebrating I think not. We are short staffed because a couple sparrows never showed up last week to their jobs here with us so we have been being thrown around and sitting far more than we did at the beginning of this disaster "vacation" assignment. I'm beyond upset because our assigned counselor Mrs.R has my book as I mentioned previously and she didn't show up not one day last week to work. This sadness, fear and anxiety she has placed on my heart is terribly painful. She has the beginning of my book y'all remember I said she was reading it and she told me which now I see was probably a flesh fib she was supposed to finish reading it last weekend. How in the world am I going to get it back. I'm terrified because those pages and these are my testimony. Please pray and I'm praying if nothing else I get the book back. Obviously if your reading it the prayers worked. My heart would be shattered that I so gracefully and obediently wrote these pages and she took them and not with care. On a more positive note y'all during our very short outside recreation first thing I saw was a big red truck and the postman pulling into this place where I am still stuck. Yep red truck with the mailman. I'm not sure if that meant my family received my letters or that my letters from them are here or that my rescue to go home is in the red, but I do know it was a heart hug from God. I kept praying that the Holy Spirit be with me and protect my daughter while I go into the last stretch of this assignment. Tomorrow which is my 45th day here and a Sunday is when we are supposed to change the color of our shirts because it's 45 in red 45 in blue and 30 in green if you're here the whole 120 days. Since I'm supposedly which now with no counselor who knows 90 days I will be departing in my blue shirt which I will hopefully be putting on this coming Thursday. We only do color changes on Thursdays. I wish we wore pink on Wednesdays. But with all the flesh sparrows out and book jackers I'm not 100% confident anything will go to what is flesh planned. Chaos and depression and fear is all that's in this devildisaster hold. Thank God I've been reading my Bible and able to hear his words to me and for me. He keeps showing me heart hugs even though my kiddo has yet to write my heart is content with what the will for my life is from God. I trust him and his plans. It's all I hold on to in here. Hope and faith with the side of prayer and a dash of Holy Spirit y'all. The Bible study ladies are both wearing then one is wearing red converse shoes y'all heart hugs in the red. I wrote that as they walked into our dorm before Bible study y'all. Then Bible study was amazing as always we read in John which I was already deep into highlighting lately and doubting Thomas. But how God and Jesus Christ continually show miraculous signs of who God is and how he loves us. We we're also asked what our Holy Spirit or purpose is if we have found it and I told the cute little Bible study ladies about my book, this book, this beloved testimony I've been preparing for y'all and my blessed self. It was yet again a divine meeting. I also need to keep praying for Mrs. R to give me back my other pages of this testimony. I wrote those by the grace of God alone. Please lord send hard hugs and miraculous works. Please in your name come rescue me soon. Side note please go into Mrs.R and have her return my book as soon as she can. Lord I wrote these words for you through you and it's how I'm going to be a willing vessel of your amazing power. I have faith and hope in you alone O Lord.

Returned mail

ARMOR OF PROTECTION. NOT ONLY WAS I PRAYING FOR GOD TO PLACE A protective shield of armor around my daughter and family but myself and my brain. A helmet of armor protecting my thoughts from the outside devil bull honkey that tries to come through. I imagine God literally coming down and placing bubble wrap, Holy Spirit bubble wrap around my daughter and family. Then I pictured him placing a beautiful helmet shield of light protection Holy Spirit hat that will ward off any bad news deviled dookie lies that tried to get through. Thank you, God, for protecting us. Loving us and allowing our minds to create such vivid signs of real protection and love. Grace and humility. My letters were returned because it was God's way of protecting my daughter from the heavy heart, I was about to place on her with my words of anxiety and fear. I have to speak kind, patient and loving y'all that letter I wrote would have crushed my daughter and my mom's spirit and brought a heavy deep sadness and sorrow to my family. I didn't realize it at the time because I was merely venting my frustrations, but God used that returned mail to guide me to a learning moment. Our words are powerful. If I don't have anything nice to say don't say anything at all. God thank you for not allowing that message to attack my daughter and my family. Thank you for disciplining me and allowing me to learn from what I had done. All the glory to you God. Ladies, we have to be careful with how we approach situations. We must be slow to speak slow to anger think about the bigger picture. Our children cannot comprehend some things that happen in our lives. We must guide them to God. Wisdom is learned and put into action with few words. We must use our words wisely. I love this teaching moment, and I hope you understand and learn something too. Encourage and empower people not place heavy stones on their open wounds.

Power of prayer

GOOD MORNING, GOOD DAY, GOOD EVENING OR GOOD NIGHT. WHENEVER you're reading this, I wish you a good moment. So, I'm sitting here at 6:45 AM. We just got back from breakfast and as I'm reading Mark one and two I was compelled to write a specific prayer. In these scriptures there are a lot of miracles that happen with healing and casting out demons. There is a lot of baptisms and preaching. So, ladies I'm sitting here just collecting my thoughts on this whole mail return situation, no letters from home and no outbound phone calls that have been made to my family. We have to completely rely on prayer. There is so much power in prayer y'all. Every time we feel overwhelmed, hurt, sad, confused, lost or condemned, we have to pray. Be quiet and listen for God's response. We get bombarded with clutter and noise on the daily no matter where we are. As much as I've been sitting here alone and not able to talk too much the devil still swarms in with clouds, lightning and loud Thunder in my soul and mind. I know you experience with this too because it's part of being in a flesh suit. That's why prayer is so incredibly important y'all. Jesus literally had to leave cities and towns and find secluded places where he could pray. So, I was moved to not only share that but to while I'm quietly on my box, sitting write a specific prayer.

Dear God please continue to wrap my family in your bubble wrap of protection while I'm still stationed where I am. Please protect each one of these beautiful ladies at my resort and their families and loved ones as well. Dear God father please continue to work on my will, assignment, plans you have for my life and all who breed this or don't. Plans that are good plans to prosper. Please take that judgment mallet and deem my stay here as you see it be fit, thy will be done. Take control take front and center of my life our lives and we will embrace your words to find the right path. Please God clothe me with your full body of armor. The helmet of, hat of the Holy Spirit on my head to protect our thoughts, our hands and feet to protect our movement, our hearts to protect our peace and soul, our mouths to protect our words and our eyes to protect our sight. Ears to protect what

124

we hear. Dear God please with your utmost grace love and honor please go in to whoever in the flesh needs to hear what you say about us. About me and my stay here where I currently am. And for the reader wherever they are. I love you more than anything for eternity, my dear God in your name I pray with hope and the fearful faith, Jesus Christ, God my ABBA Amen.

Empower and encourage

....

HAPPY SUNDAY LADIES OR AGAIN HAPPY WHATEVER DAY OF THE WEEK IT is you are reading this. I pray you slept well ate good and feel full of the Holy Spirit heart hugs. If I'm writing this testimony it means I'm still here in my final flock. I don't dream to much here but last night I had several pretty vivid dreams aside from waking up multiple times to go potty. I was in a weird place with brown doors and cabinets and narrow hallways. I found myself seated on a white stallion horse saddleless. The horse would gallop but my ride with him was anything but bumpy. I didn't need to even grab his mane. It was like a glide on silk. It felt smooth and stress free. Then I woke up far before lights would be turned on, but that just gave me time to have my intimate morning conversation with my father. Then as soon as I'm sharing my dream at recreation outside on this beautiful day the lord gave us, it hit me. I finally fully trust the Lord. God is in complete control of my world. After sharing my accountability and plowing parts of my heart and heart flesh I was able to breathe and let go trust God trust that he alone has my life, my sentence, my everything under his divine control. My dream confirmed this. As I shared it, I felt it. Then ladies I ran 20 laps around our track. Then I did 120 push-ups. Y'all I am not a runner, but I feel so free and blessed that why wouldn't I want to run when I can. Use my energy and soak in that thing they call a runners high. I finally found that. I felt light on my feet and gliding with the Holy Spirit. Ladies, these moments are precious. Each time we are woken up for a new day is a blessing. Thank God for all the tiny miracles he does in our lives each day ladies. For the legs, feet and endurance to be able to run. For the shoes on our toes. For our tiny toes. I had a good heart conversation with one of my best friends too. She said, how are you always in a good mood and happy when I know how much you miss Madison. I said because God placed my purpose inside me to encourage and empower people. I gave and give him continually my fears and worries so that I can be that willing vessel of God's powerful love and words shared. I found my ultimate purpose in this place y'all are seeing it through these pages. I told her she's getting a front row seat, in person live and in action. She's my flock best friend. I want her to feel what I've been feeling. She smiled and I wish I could hug her, when we are free from this flock I know she will be a forever friend. I love her and I love you too ladies. Hug all the people in your world if you can. Because when that little gesture gets taken away it does not feel flesh good. But what does is sharing this testimony with you and living it with her. I love you Kritty we've got this.

GodSidence

LADIES I GOT TO SPEAK TO MY AMAZING DAUGHTER ON THE PHONE TODAY. This was an answered prayer times a lot. Not only is she good, great she's holding the fort down while I'm at this final flock. I've been praying so hard for her to have the bubble wrap Holy Spirit protection around her and God is confirming she is OK. I pray he continues to protect her and guide her in the right way she should go. He also protected her and myself by removing certain situations and people while I'm here. I guess God's rejection is his way of protection. I just wanted to know Maddie my daughter was OK and she is. The rest of it is up to God. I will say God is good all the time y'all. Allowing me to hear her voice was all I needed to make it to the rest of the days I have here. But it doesn't hurt to ask to be rescued now more than ever to go be with my baby girl. So God please in your name before anything gets out of control please come and rescue me from this final flock so that I could be there in person for my daughter. Your will be done in her life and mine. Your plans are becoming more and more clear as the days go by. But only you know when my time at this assignment will be over. The flesh said July 11th 2024 but I know you may have an earlier departure up your sleeve. The judge flesh said sixty days and I'm surpassing that. So please Lord allow the flesh to deem my completion of this program complete far sooner than July 11th. You will know when my daughter will need me most. Please Lord I cry and beg for you to protect her but also now more than ever to come from my rescue. My heart flesh knows my daughter needs me home. She's been brave and strong on her own for a while. Please go into the flesh who has control of my stay here and deem me done. Let me go home to my beautiful daughter. Sisters ladies nothing happens by accident. I believe all things happen for a reason. God's timing is impeccable, divine and his. This goes for lessons learned, sentence being given, sowing and reaping what we sow, our relationships and pretty much every GodSidence in between y'all. It took me a little longer to fall asleep last night because I was conversing and praying to my father. That Holy Spirit bubble wrap is so essential for my daughter and mom. Then I was led to pray over for my sister. My flesh sister I had another dream the other day about a white SUV and being at the gas station and I got gas in my mouth. But what I've gathered from thinking clearly about it is my sister needs to be in my life she will be the one to pick me up from this final flock in her white car so the signs of red exit and the bright white light represent the water and the blood of Jesus and my rescue. But the gas in the dream represents my sister's choices of drinks, which I am supposed to gracefully lead her to recovery and healing from. I was also moved to say she's a fantastic writer as well and she will be collaborating with me on other life happenings or one of her own. Y'all God is so good. She was the one going with me to my court dates and even wanted to bring me to the last one on March 20th. But God had bigger things in store for all of us. Myself, my daughter, my mom, my sister and my family. No wonder finding nemo was on so much and all these little signs of my sister. Her name in the sober tree, her name in my recovery bible. My vivid dreams about her. I once walked in her shadow but now we will stand together. United and better than we have ever been. Y'all I can't wait to hug my flesh sister, my daughter and my mom. God is good. Be patient while he works miracles in our lives. Your life when given over to God is going to be more than you will ever know ladies. I am a walking, writing and breathing testimony of this. God's will for my life is turning out to be so much more than I ever imagined. I love you God so so so much now get your pen out and start documenting your life for Jesus ladies. Spread the good news. Educate yourself with scripture. Be wise, be patient, be kind and most of all love everyone the way God loves you.

My daughter braved me

Y'ALL I WOKE UP AT 3:00 AM AND HAD SOME PRETTY EMOTIONAL TEARS flowing from my tired eyes. They were mixed emotions from grace, gratefulness, fear and affirmation. God put it on my heart another, thy will be done assignment confirmation, not only for me to encourage and empower women but to become the best mom I can. To get out of here and help her complete her GED program, help her practice driving and show her she is first in my world. No man or other human takes her place. Also to teach her about her father God. She already spoke about God on the phone conversation that we had. Ladies as I've wrote about before as parents, as mothers it is our biggest responsibility to lead our children to the word of God. Be the footprints of God our daughters can walk in behind us. My daughter has no idea how her courage made me willing and able to be courageous in here. Her laugh and voice braved me through the phone. Plus I was comforted that no matter what happens outside of here God is and always will protect my daughter and family. We have to continue praying for our loved ones and putting our trust in the Lord. Daily, hourly and every minute. Y'all it helps your heart have peace. Then I was thinking of all the heart hugs I've received in here, the food on my plates that Maddie would enjoy, the flock mate in here with her name, Madison. The movie with the daughters named Maddie. Watching the barbie movie, inside out and letters to God. The red cars driving by, the number 4, the GED class because Madi needs her GED. The younger flock mate that has her attitude. My flock mates and sparrows with daughters her age getting their permits and driving. Those conversations about their daughters until now I didn't realize we're led by the holy spirit. We were speaking about our daughters because God is working in all of our lives and theirs. Our lives your life soul sister, be courageous like our kiddos are. Let go and let God. I know 100% how difficult that is because I was abruptly, temporarily removed from my daughters life March 20th with absolutely no warning. It's now June 13th at 6:50 AM and I'm sitting on my blue box with peace and content in my flesh heart. God is and will protect our children. Keep the hope alive. Gain the knowledge from the Bible and wisdom from God's words. Share them, imprint them on your heart and soul so you can imprint them on your daughters, your nieces, nephews grandbabies whoever. Then remember who is in the control room, our father! Trust him he won't let us sink. Ladies this place i'm assigned to has transformed my heart into a feather comforter. Cloud of love and kindness. Grace and forgiveness. Take a moment to reflect on what's happening in your life be still and know God is your redeemer. He is working diligently in your heart and world for good. For your daughters for good. Then when your divine rescue comes the fireworks explosion there's only one name to praise. That's Jesus. All the bible study moments with the songs my daughter and I love. All the commercials that reminded me of her. The tiny mini miracles y'all. Don't overlook those many moments. Or small heart hugs. Rainbows, smells, sounds, conversations, names, people, colors GED classes, glasses, food on your plate heart hugs. Those are what the Holy Spirit shows us to comfort our hearts. Empower and encourage us to keep going. I'm going to be the best mom ever to my daughter when I am rescued. Best daughter to my mother. Best daughter to my God my father. Best version of who God has ultimately made me to be. I'm listening, I'm observing, I'm acquiring knowledge and wisdom. Ladies let's be the best moms we can be. We deserve to feel and know our value. We are beautiful and brave. No matter what the world throws our way, sentences, jail time, probation, divorce, separation, the loss of a loved one, hurt, fear or depression. Let's grab on to God's robe, his hand, his heart and his words and let's brave ourselves ladies. This flock has literally saved me. Braved me and broke me little bits at a time. Our futures are bright y'all. Now God send that rainbow I'm supposed to ride out onto my daughter and mom. Please delay no further. I'm done being a caterpillar I want to fly like that beautiful butterfly.

Denial

I WAS IN DENIAL IF I THOUGHT I COULD DRINK AND MAINTAIN A HEALTHY relationship. I don't have the desire to even drink, but I felt the need to do some plowing. Some inventory of my heart. Every relationship I had was affected either directly or indirectly with alcohol. Never for the good either. I admit to you, my father and all those are hurt along the way. It wasn't just that bad car accident on January 12, 2021. It was drinking from the devil's cup, and then letting all my morals go. Letting a false sense of confidence, a false sense of control, a false reality that I wasn't the problem. Yes, ladies, it's me. I'm the problem. Especially when I drink from the devil's cup. My mouth becomes toxic. My heart becomes hardened and stubborn. My choices become led by the devil. No more ever again. I would accuse and let my thoughts straight toward negative. I wouldn't admit when I was wrong. Get lost, Satan and thank you God for showing me that I was in denial before. I've learned so much about me. Ladies, be honest with yourself, be open, be brave. God already knows our deepest darkest secrets. We can't hide from him ever. It feels good to take personal inventory before our God. Y'all do it try it. Even if you don't want to share in a public testimony like I have, at least pray about it. Tell a close loved one. It's healing. We are human. We will make mistakes. It's how we learn and grow from them that makes the difference. God forgives us y'all. So take responsibility for our actions. Be courageous. Be free.

Camera check

CAMERA CHECK WITHOUT THE CAMERA. WOW SO THAT WAS A VERY interesting group session. We just had with a devil puppet counselor. Now I will take accountability for not being so holy or godly with my words sometimes or thinking about how they will affect someone. Also, sometimes the truth hurts. So our counselor started out as she always does poking the bear and belittling us flock mates and certain ones in particular. One whom stood up for herself, but then, since the a lot of counselor felt at a loss of words, I was brought to the center of the group for camera check. Yep for everyone to let me know how they think I should focus on my recovery. God, I know you are the only source way in recovery life but I had no choice, but to take my seat in the center of the 32 Female Circle, and devil, puppet counselor. She told me I was rehearsed, two polished and like a speaker on an evangel TV show. That of which I have no clue who or what that means. But I took the constructive criticism from my flock mates with Grace because I do say things out of spunk and sometimes my humor can be morbid. Sorry ladies, but being locked up with 32 females will do a thing or two to your hormones and your mouth. But I took accountability for what I said, which was that one of the flock mates was crying wolf. I only say this because we had a conversation when I first arrived at this final flock and she was trying to get MTR or released in anyway possible medically. The other day they took her to the hospital because she said she ate bad Food. It was a bad hotdog mind you all 32 of us eat exactly the same food every day. She ended up coming back just fine, yes, I prayed even though I could see through what was really happening. Needless to say, I apologized directly to her, but the counselor still had a devil agenda. Basically I'm too skinny. I'm not that into God and I'm too polished improper. My words are too educated and rehearsed like I flocking excuse my flock French knew I was coming to this place so I could be part of this devildisaster hole production of some sort. But I prayed during this camera check and After and God is good. I held my composure up there and displayed great leadership qualities. Even though the stones being thrown were lit with fire and hate. I praise my God, my father for all he has done for me and showing me my purpose in this place. Another cognitive lesson learned. I, Natalie can be brave and speak of my God, even in front of a not so deserving audience. Ladies that camera check was an inhumane and meant to steal kill and destroy a part of me and my light. I'll tell you what though if my God is for me, no one can be against me. I'm taking accountability for my actions. I'm plowing my heart. I'm constantly taking moral inventory of my wrongful doings. So buzz off, you devil puppet counselor I'll pray for you and your job position and how you should too find the words that describe you. Maybe she needs a camera check, to sit in the hot seat, mask off outside clothes taken no makeup no mail no love from human flesh heart hugs. Let's see how brave she could be.

Finish strong

APPROACHING THE FINISH LINE, COMPLETING AN ASSIGNMENT, GETTING a promotion are all ways I've looked at this whole experience. What started off as a blindsided arrest played out to be an awakening of my whole life through Jesus Christ and God himself. Y'all I'm runner up to the next few ladies who will be departing this devilcation and I'm wrapping up all the loose ends. My integrity, humility, grace, kindness, empathy and forgiveness have merely tripled doubled, increased beyond Infinity. My love, respect, honor and trust have skyrocketed. Y'all through God alone was I able to surrender my life in this flock and my daughters and families. Y'all know from reading it, it wasn't easy. But with God alone prayer I have relinquished my life my will and placed it in God's divine hands of authority. Holy moly testimony all glory to God, he is good all the time. Don't give up right before the blessing the big finale. See it through to the last millisecond. Finish the race proud and brave, strive to get an A+ not a mediocre C minus, become the eloquent polished rehearsed through god boss B word you've earned, that certificate is from God. All the praise and glory will be to him alone. He is the cornerstone, saving grace, fireworks, promotion you've been working so hard for. Diamonds are made under pressure ladies. Let's shine bright for Jesus well polished and refined.

Answered prayers

ANSWERED PRAYERS ON GOD'S TIME Y'ALL THIS HAS BEEN A JOURNEY. AS my days are now on the decline in time here I had one of my last times to make a phone call today. Yep y'all at first no one answered. I felt a sense of peace though because I've learned to breathe and go pray. As I'm finishing up my prayer on my blue treasure box, Mr. Abad called me out again. Mind you I just finished writing my dear God letter. I left the office of Mr. Abad with the best feeling ever. Joy, peace, and comfort with love. God has been moving in my family's life this whole time. Just as I have prayed for. Ladies don't give up on a prayer and faith. God sends us hard hugs and signs for a reason. Be still and know, he's working in our lives our kids and our families. My mom has no idea how happy I was to finally hear her voice after 90 days. God I wanna personally praise you and thank you. All the glory will be to you alone God. Remember that ladies when you feel the devil sneak in believe and pray God will and does answer prayers on his divine time. Miracles happen every day I'm living and breathing, this proof of God's amazing glory all the praise and worship to him alone, ladies.

Just keep smiling

Y'ALL WE HAVE TO EMPOWER EACH OTHER LOVE ONE ANOTHER LIFE IS FAR too short to bully and neglect or discriminate. Plus it makes god sad makes me sad makes you sad let's make each other smile. Smile the biggest and the deepest in the darkest storms. Imagining that rainbow I'm gonna slide home on to my Maddie and my family. Wasn't there rainbows in Mrs. Frizzle's magic school bus adventures? I'm going to have to watch those when I get home. Just an update on the shorts thing I was moved to put in a grievance I didn't name names I'm praying for whoever made those roles. I'm praying if I just heard what i think i heard if i fill this notebook up and write on all the pages they will take it because you can only have two notebooks in your property. Ohh, No one is taking my paper away from me y'all that's ridiculous the lord will not let that happen. God i trust the plans you have for my life please come and heart hug the doo doo out of me during outside recreation. Heart hugged spirit cat. Y'all we were outside in a cute kitty was tiptoeing across the field and yet again. They are awful here y'all. But i took it as a heart hug spirit cat style. My cat's at home or my kitten therapy i missed them. Then when we sat down for rack up box sets loud fighter jets flew over yet again making it very apparent to my ears my Lord is sending that army to save me. Sooner than later period ladies this life, flock life, home life, jail life, work life is hard. But no matter where you find yourself in life stay close to the lord. Stay obedient to lord read his word his testimony period don't let the devil puppets and devil sparrows even so as pierce your soul or heart. They can touch your flesh or her ear exterior no one can touch what God calls his.

Wisdom

THE BENEFITS OF WISDOM Y'ALL I'M GOING TO AGAIN READ PROVERBS AND tried to articulate it as the Lord puts it on my heart to share. The first verse in proverbs 2: 1 is my child listened to what I say and treasure my commands. Tune your ears to wisdom and concentrate on understanding. #3 cry out for insight and ask for understanding. Wow y'all i just had a heart hug like no other after showers i put my shower items into my treasure chest then sat back down to read proverbs i saw psalms 144: 7 reached down from heaven and rescued me; Rescue me from deep waters from the power of my. Their mouths are full of lies they swear to tell the truth but they lie instead. Ohh my heart squeezed y'all. That is going to be my favorite new verse tune in my head melody to my madness in this flock y'all. Read that again I'll write it again so you have to read it again to proceed. Psalms 144: 7 through 8 reached out from heaven and rescued me from deep waters from the power of my enemies their mouths are full of lies they swear to tell the truth but they lie instead. Not really take that in girls, ladies, grandma's, sisters, whoever you are believe that verse and take it to heart period make it the only truth way in life period our god our father is sending out that army to save us each one of us exactly where we are.

Preparation Visualization

He will save me from this flock you from a flock, from the darkness and bring you into light. Stay focused on him and the heart hugs will continue throughout your journey. It's cute that I was thinking about when I get to type this testimony out be at home with my cats when I'm doing the recordings on my voice for the audio book my kitties are part of it. Ohh to hear their cute little purrs and meows period that spirit cat made my morning she was looking right at me then all the heart huge scriptures that were placed on my heart to read and sh He gives justice to the oppressed and food to the hungry the Lord frees the prisoners. Praise the Lord y'all Amen Hallelujah holy moly testimony I was crying as I wrote those words. Then I look up again and all the flock mates are facing the TV, backs towards me. I'm weeping reading the promises of the Lord which is way more exciting than whatever is on that TV. I can't believe how settled my heart feels I can't tell if my tears are excited happy or safe to your house. All of the above. Psalms 144 seven reached down from heaven and rescue me rescue me from deep waters from the power of my enemies. God is so good all the time you all.

Proverbs 4:4 My father taught me take my words to heart follow my commands and you will live. Another fighter fight jet flew over this morning y'all I take those as heart hugs. Even though it's probably just that we are near an Air Force training base they are my heart hugs. Then they were taking a roll call for those who need their GED and it made me think of my daughter Maddie bug. She's signed up at home online and she also. I don't want to lose out all these vital moments plus expanding her love for the lord. I want to plant great seeds in her heart about our father the lord is our father he is good all the time. I am to instruct my children in the way of the Lord and I can't do this from this flock. I can't even hug her from this flock. See her or talk to her it's actually insane. But ladies the Lord has a plan and with all these scriptures on my heart feels at peace knowing my rescue is coming soon I can feel it in my bones. I just don't know when I should get too excited because I don't want to flock fool myself again. So,

I'll recite my new favorite verse y'all that's a firework heart hug heart hook explosion psalms 146 seven he gives justice to the oppressed and food to the hungry, the Lord frees the prisoners. On the way to chow y'all with these new wonderful I recited it all the way to lunch and all the way back.

Flesh group

FLESH GROUP REALLY CARES ABOUT FINALLY GOT MY FOLDER FOR MY loose leaf pages from my book and the start of Heart hug then y'all we had a fire alarm go off. That's interesting right, fire trucks are red y'all. I can't write until after group she's already trying to say that I belong in this flock and I'm not a child of God. I had to bite my lip ladies this is not going to be well and sometimes we have to go through things and oppression from people who have control over us but just know they're playing with words not us. She's also saying she's the light in this room I am just using Jesus cards. Y'all I even tried sitting away from her you won't be able to see my handwriting because this is typed but it is bad because I'm shaking and she's trying to crush my spirit. I told her that I am a child of God and I am different. The Lord knows the plans he has for me and you ladies even though we may have to sit in a circle and be judged and persecuted. You don't have to take it in or merely even listen to the flesh sparrow suit. God will rescue you and me from our enemies those who persecute you. Just continue to know who your father is and know that you are forgiven and know nothing of what she says is true. Lord let me hear only your words about me. Ladies don't let the flesh devil words affect you. It's clear to me now why I read those certain scriptures that I did before this session. I thank you Lord and I love you and I trust you.

Oppressing counselor

THE COUNSELOR WAS THROWING STONES AT ME TO SEE IF I WOULD CHANGE my way of thinking to believe what she was saying was true. I only believe what the Lord says about me. So, I actually thank you Lord that was an obedience test I am faithful to you Lord. I tried to bring your name and your Holy Spirit into the room and conversation, and she took the baton and bashed me with it. I took solid stance and my ground on how I believe ladies. I was not trying to say I'm better than anyone we are all different you, me and her. This group session happened exactly the way it was meant to to prove that if you are obedient to the Lord he will come rescue you from earth from the deep dark waters. Be obedient he said these words in psalms. He sets prisoners free, don't let the flesh suit or any flesh suit put things on your heart that are untrue. I'm so glad I brought my book to write during group that was a heart hug y'all. This was all the Lords doing; he ensured I had the tools to record the wrongful doing of flesh suits. I love you ladies we are in this together I'm in no place to judge anyone due to my past choices but the Lord has given me the armor, the tools, the patience to help empower us and myself through this. To show you if you honor your Lord, your God, your father and you believe in him wholeheartedly he will save you.

Catwalk talks

WHILE WALKING TO CHOW I CONTINUALLY REPEATED THOSE VERSES from psalms and proverbs. Then I saw a red car drive by again ladies I'm not sure about the red color yet but I'm documenting it just in case something amazing happens. So as I'm walking and talking to the Lord in my head I'm praying for that whole situation that just happened towards us at counseling group. I prayed for this sparrow whom tried to damage my heart and soul and knowledge for that matter. For our father to go into her heart and heal whatever is weighing heavy on her soul. I can tell it's something hard and heavy I also prayed he send her heart hugs. We have to pray for our enemies and those who try to hurt us. People who hurt want you to hurt too. I wish that on no one I merely was trying to be honest and open and I'm lied about and to with her word play ladies, don't do that to your sisters. Even if you've been given flesh power or authority always go into a situation the Lord top of mind and love like he does. What fun is it to knowingly hurt someone in a group of people just because you can because you're not wearing a colored shirt. You're allowed to pluck your own eyebrows and do your hair and put on makeup. But what if all that was taken away from you and you can no longer hide behind whatever mask you built up that Shields what's really going on. Being vulnerable in front of 24 other women is hard enough but then to shame accuse and lie about her because her insecurities is just painful period ladies and honestly I promise you won't feel good inside after you do that. You'll go back to whatever bad habit or addiction you may be covering up. Back to the bottle or that burger and fries or that needle. Because now not only are you still hurting you know you hurt someone else. If we walk with the Lord in our spirit and hearts the words that come out of our mouth will be nothing but positive and true. I promise if you pray before you have a counseling session, a long talk with your kids, your husband your dad your teacher whoever I know the Lord will put on your soul the right words to say. Girls and they won't be what was done to me today. What happened so much in here is insane and maybe it's happened to you too. I'm praying for you right now I pray the Lord sends hard hugs directly where you are reading this. Unfortunately what should be part of a recovery program is a spirit crusher but don't worry ladies you're God's got you.

God first

LADIES IT'S FRIDAY NIGHT ON THIS END OF THE PAGES AND I'M JUST IN shock looking back and reflecting on my whole experience here at this flock. I've learned a lot but not how you would have thought. By reading my Bible and being observant and noticing heart hugs and heart pain, bad counseling and Jesus counseling. Ultimately Jesus has been my father, my ABBA, my dad, my teacher, my counselor, my support, my best friend, my protector, my guidance and my peace through this whole experience. I would not have made it through a week without him or this whole time. I literally have been in direct conversation with the Lord 24 hours a day since March. I believe more than ever he is the only way all those times I wrote about that should have crushed me only didn't because he put the Holy Spirit in me to write my testimony about it. I will always and I mean always ladies put God as #1 in everything in my life. He is first he's always for Infinity. I know the plans he has for me are good, the plans he has for you ladies are good too. All you have to do is believe and say I trust you Lord, I love you and I'm so grateful for all you have done for us. Then continue like I said to be patient and obedient and get schooled on the Bible. For heaven's sakes I'll put out the Jesus card whenever I want who even says that ladies. Y'all, I wrote so much I ran out of ink from the blue pen I was using. Talk about being inked. I think I used to have the same pins in school for well the whole four years unless I lost them. How incredible I've never used a whole pen before. I feel like I just accomplished something y'all. Ladies I have that pen that was used to write this beloved book my testimony for you the reader. Even if you don't read this I'm still praying for you sister. Even after another wrongful accusing session after my prayers were going up even during it only because the Lord put it on my heart to be able to be brave and strong in these storms. I really pray ladies that you find it in your hearts to be brave and bold and be different. You've read through this testimony so far you have read about the heart hugs you have been having your own as well. The most important thing you need to do is believe. Believe in the Lord as your savior I am father.

Believe he sent his son to die on the cross. Believe the Holy Spirit is now with you and for you. You have eternal life ladies. He won't leave you in a place of pain too long he won't let the flesh suits touch your soul. He will save you from your flock, from yourself, from pain, from homelessness, from jail, from wrongful doings, from false accusations and from being stoned and persecuted. Just believe.

Exit

....

It's 8:00 AM on Saturday morning and this girl woke up at 4:20 AM y'all. Y'all you're not allowed to have any movement until the lights are turned on so I prayed and talked to my father the Lord for pretty much 4 hours. This is not a schedule that is beneficial to anyone. If you're awake you should be able to work, workout clean whatever healthy habit you would like. I will always grab this book first thing in the morning. So good flocking morning during my talk with god this morning I literally noticed the exit sign is red y'all. I promise it's been there the whole time but for some heart hug reason this morning it's the bright light I saw beaming by the door. Bright red exit. Heart hug in the red. Then about I don't know 3 or 30 minutes later I saw a bright light y'all there's no outside light that comes in here but I was staring at the wall as I was talking to God and a tinkerbell like light walked up the wall and far higher than even if there was a window light could come through. Y'all heart hug I had a lot of them this morning from the exit sign to that tinker bell fairy light to the bright red folder I saw them passing around in the office at around 7:00 AM. I also had an epiphany to share after chow and a chance for more heart hugs to happen so I will meet pen to paper after the catwalk. Today is also 4/20 I was locked away 320days ago and this is the 120th page. Heart hug in the 20s I also started doing 20 push-ups y'all. Maybe I'm just bored or maybe their heart hugs from the Lord.

Fighter jets

EVERY TIME I HEAR THEM I SMILE AND SAY IN MY HEAD I WILL RESCUE you. Jesus will send out an army to find me in the middle of the darkest night is true, I will rescue you. Miss Soto is 77 years old she is the counselor teaching the session today. She is tiny with long hair sweet spirit, fragile and dainty. We are currently watching a video on inhalants and honestly don't get me wrong it was good information, but I never knew how to even use inhalants and there were videos on how to sniff, huff, bag and whip it. Don't forget poppers that were used to increase sexual enhancement. Y'all I'm so not a drug dealer or inhaler I would never even put nasal spray up my nose. In any case it was a very educational film and now when i get home i'm going to ask my daughter if she knew about inhalers. Apparently kids and teens are the ones taking our household cleaning products and gasoline or vegetable spray and inhaling it to get a high or hallucination. No ma'am y'all if you know what these are and are partaking in the huffing and puffing please don't blow your house down. Put the inhalant down and let's get natural high on watching our babies grow up. Let's pray for our kiddos who are exposed to this experience and keep their brains from getting rocked any more than they already do in this crooked and messed up world. Just an observation all the green shirts are sleeping or slumped down in their chairs.

Red's blues greens oh my

NOT SURE THAT IS WHAT REDS ARE SUPPOSED TO BE LOOKING UP TO. Again I don't think this is about learning or recovery it's about following rules and waiting out your allotted days 90 to 180. It's clear to me every day just being here I guarantee right after this inhalant class the TV is going on and everyone will migrate to whatever movie or show is on. I of course will be sitting on my box finishing my proofreading and being obedient to what the Holy Spirit places on my heart to share with you ladies. We are released to the day room and the rest of the flock is watching TV. I need to catch up on my proofreading then get deep into my Bible again, so I'll be back to these pages in a split minute. Today I finally proofread my entire testimony and as I was reading it, I just got heart hugged several times on how to release and share this testimony with the world. I listened to a lot of audio books and I feel like I will need to be the one to read this in that type of form as well as an actual beautiful paperback. I am a lover of feeling, touching and smelling a book weird I know y'all. But I also think in order to get the full effect of the tone and the vibe of the testimony my raspy spunky voice will need to articulate these dear pages in audio book form. As I reread or actually read it only once in my head and sometimes out loud to myself it will definitely have a better shock value and be personal if you can hear it straight from the source. Me. Y'all that was a heart hug because I can't wait to be out and collaborate with what Madi has been doing through this and my mom and my sisters. It will be a nice little gateway or bridge to either another book altogether or a mallet striking these very pages as complete. We will see what the Lord places on my soul. I'm sitting here ladies trying to be moved on my next words but I'm being called to open the Bible. Hold up ladies there is a shirt assignment ceremony that just happened. Y'all this isn't OK it's merely based off how long you've been here and if you got written up. My heart is hurting for the girls who thought they were moving up and then who thought they were green and went to orange. Orange means that you are in trouble. How heartbreaking belittling and ridiculous ladies. I wish they didn't hold on so tight to those shirt colors. If you're following the lord girls you'll be in green in his name the whole time you're here. This just goes to show you not to let the flesh suits or sparrows call you anything other than beautiful, brave and a daughter to the one and only judge our creator Jesus Christ. If you have the Holy Spirit in you who absolutely cares what the flesh says. Even when one of them was asked what does the blue shirt mean to her she didn't have the right response and she still got it. Whereas the other flock mate is young two and kind of has the same personality and she was told she was on hold. Ladies that's why you have to open your Bible and believe God is the only thing with the keys and colored shirts to your life. I wish I could just stop this ceremony of flesh judgment and say I want to wear a rainbow shirt. I am the rainbow shirt of my flock. That's seriously exactly what the Lord put on me to write. Then I walked my three sized shoes too big Crocs to the crayons it's set up in here like a preschool I used to teach out at church I got a red, orange, yellow, green, blue and purple crayon. This place won't take my immense love for rainbows away. Every rule, every Sparrow, every flesh suit mother flocker in this place can shove that shirt ceremony up their flock hole. I can't stop smiling because this is not only a flocking great testimony because ladies you watch the fireworks will be soon and then jaws will drop and I'll be the talk of the flock because I told them I'm praying my way out of here and who knows what color I'll be in.

Walk the walk talk the talk

I DON'T WANT TO APRIL FOOL MYSELF AGAIN AND BE FLOCK FOOLED BUT I also got a red snow cone thing today. Remember the red vehicles matching mine. And the lady with the bright red bracelet. I would be flock famous for my love and obedience to the lord. I wonder if something like that happened, would the meaning of the colors change. In peer group the girls all wrote on a card pros and cons for each flock mate and mine was all about Jesus and my love for the Lord in cons y'all cons were that I may be too nice to people and I'm too positive. What the actual flock y'all. I'm merely doing what my Lord and savior has moved me to do no one is making me it's in me. This is who I am. I love you ladies the reader I love all these ladies even the ones who probably whisper about me. I love you all. I love you soul sister, I love the monitors and I'm praying for them as well. And I'm not making it up, the Lord knows my true feelings and heart. Y'all if you're this far into my testimony and a moment crosses your mind that you think I could even make this up any of it you're flocking insane. So in proofreading y'all I need to take the F word out. I so freely throw around out of my mouth I need to not put it in my book. That was not godly of me so I will fix it. The words flipping or flocking sound way cuter anyway. Now I don't even know how to speak I'm so twisted like a twizzler. Anyway, ladies the council's departed and well my counselor didn't meet with me today I guess I flocking got fib too. It's OK my only counselor, savior, judge, father that has authority over my life is already working on my behalf. And he's doing it for you ladies too. Heart hug y'all he's working on yours and mine. If you're still with me in this journey I know you're feeling heart hugs, laughs, epiphanies and unfortunately challenges and sadness, loneliness and maybe some regret or guilt. But I'm here to tell you there may be pain in tears at night but joy comes in the morning. And n those super hard heart wrenching heartful dark moments just pray. If you can out loud but if you're in a place like where I have to be mute pray silently. Either way he sees you, he hears you, he loves you,

you are not lost in his eyes. He's coming to rescue you. I just laughed to myself because I really don't say much here just I thought about forgetting how to speak. But no y'all I'm loud and proud. I've always been told my voice carries and you better believe it will it's about to carry this testimony, the lord's love for us come with the holy spirit shining through me louder than I've ever been before. That's an exciting feeling, don't cover your ears though. I'll be respectful of your eardrums. I just want y'all to know the love of the Lord that I've been feeling and been shown through the heart hugs from the Holy Spirit. It's something incredible and worth the loud octaves. It's so hard not to speak out loud more. The Lord has taught me so flocking much and I'm holding this so close to my heart I will continue to deep dive into that Bible and claim it as my new cell phone, GPS, Google search. Y'all, I haven't had a phone in a hot minute and I haven't needed one to fall in love with my father and learn the best most important lessons in life. That he the Lord our God sent his son Jesus to die on the cross for our sins. Then I asked beg the Holy Spirit to come into me over and over again and the blessings of knowledge have been abundant and fantastic. The Bible is his words for us when you need a friend to talk to, text open the Bible and talk to Luke Matthew or the Romans. If you are lost and not sure which way to go the Bible will plant your feet to move your spirit where you need to go. Find that good soil to be emerged into so your seeds will be planted and flourished. Next, Google search the Bible contains all knowledge. Read any story about what's going on in your life and somebody else has already walked those paths, fought the battles, asked the questions. Y'all the Bible is the Lord's testimony what the flock it's the only book you should need, you should want and you should desire to yearn learn deeply into. It's changed my life it's kept me afloat in my flocks. Y'all I thought I was reading the bible in the free but I read it and tried to get my streaks if you have the bible app you know what i mean. It's kind of like the shirt colors here wanting the credit and color change but not understanding the meaning of the color. I would read the verse of the day or even some plans as they are called but I didn't always understand why as long as I got my streaks though. No once I got my flocks that Bible purpose reading changed. And man was it worth it I have created a deeply rooted routine, habit way of flocking life through my father the lord Jesus Christ. I understand what i'm reading and when i don't i pray for my father to send the heart hug holy spirit to dummy it down for me. And here it is as I learned I taught y'all as i made it through the real bible streaksI documented them. Holy heart hug streaks.

The purpose

Not only did I create the ultimate amazing habit and routine of trusting my father the Lord he taught me patience, wisdom, obedience, reward and love. A love only he could show me in these mini storms of flock life. That's agape love y'all it's the main purpose of this life to learn, obey and be obedient to the lord. Then to spread that good news. Such scriptures were placed on my heart to read and share yesterday as you may remember and if not ladies the book is yours so flip back as you wish or don't. So, either welcome back or still hello we just made our way back into the flock dorm and we are boxed up to wait the hour and a half it takes for all now 25 plus ladies to shower up. I love this time because this is when pen meets paper. So, ladies at about 6:30 or 7:00 AM I was looking around and deep in conversation with my father my heart is filled with a peaceful purpose and my eyes filled with warm salty tears. I finally knew what I'm supposed to do when I fly free from this flock. Not only first and foremost am I supposed to continue and increase and expand my love and knowledge about my God my father my ABBA and share the good news via whatever Ave. is presented, this book my mouth the Bible the church my home my life will be led solely and purposely for him. My Lord and savior but y'all the big finale is to my one and only Madison Jean. Yep, God first, then the rest of the heart hugs were for her. Y'all my daughter is a firecracker sour patch kid light of my life. She's beautiful she's brave and she's mine for the time the Lord our father has given me to share her. I thank him for that for knowing her learning language as well as mine. You see it's always been inside that little girl to respect and love and care about her Mama. She is only 16 at the moment so she doesn't always know how to express these feelings and y'all I wasn't always the best person or mom I could be. I apologized to her on the phone and my first flock had actually sent her a letter with a skittle spit made rainbow because there were no crowns in the pre flop. Needless to say I was looking around this morning and I remember the school buses and the Sparrow who came in to ask about some of the younger ladies GED. Y'all Maddie is enrolled in an at your own pace GED program that I was not enforcing because our lives were a bit scrambled before my flocks. Yes I was sober and working but I lacked the knowledge and skills I ever so thankfully acquired here in my final flocks. The Lord gave me a daughter for the sole purpose to guide her through his way. Plus y'all I said above he knew her learning language and in order for her to really trust the process listen be encouraged and respect me and my words and knowledge I had to be temporarily removed from the scene. I know she's been trying to listen to the Lord and be brave at home when I'm not there because I begged her to open that Bible and talk to God and pray me out of my flocks. Ladies this little girl has been through a lot her flesh father is not the sharpest crayon in the box and he has done and said some things towards me in front of her and sadly to her about herself. He's merely a devil's puppet dad. I'm here to school her and brave her on the love and sin free life our father has waiting for her. That little girl has not only seen the flesh falsely accused and physically abuse me, she's also seen the flesh suit judges and lawyers and people you think our family or friends. But I know that little Madi bug knows the truth about her mama because of the way i would not fight back. Yep ladies that's the way i meant to say it not fight back. Her first instinct from her flesh father's side of the gene pool is anger and hurting people. I've tried imprinting my ways of just do good by the Lord and pray for those who persecute you because the Lord has the ultimate say in the end. Even during this time of traumatic separation from her I hope she learns the value of her words respect and empathy. From the last couple phone conversations I had with not only her but my mom she's abundantly learning that I meant more to her than what she may have been portraying through her teenage hormones. Ladies, girls, sisters, moms, aunts, grandmas and soul sisters we are all here to love one another. If you see a sister struggling a child a grandma a Sparrow a flesh suit a devil puppet grab their hand and let them know you care, you'll listen, you'll love without condition. My daughter, your daughters our daughters need us to be the best daughters of Christ God our father that we can be. If it takes putting one of you or both of you in a flock take the time to put in the work to learn educate brave love and expand your hearts and minds for the love of Jesus has for us. The sin problem was solved long ago. God did it through his son. John 3:16 for God so loved the world that he gave his one and only son. By continually gravitating towards your Bible when you have an issue or a question or thought sometimes just a moment to yourself instead of a cell phone TV or a bad habit addiction or devil puppet, you'll begin to change your life and your ways. Create the Bible habit pull out that Jesus card ladies because that's the devil's puppet playing with your words. If you believe in God and you're listening to your father no Sparrow can turn what you say into a lie. God knows the truth.

The Commencement

THIS WAS NOT A TEST, NOT A DRESS REHEARSAL. BEING INSTANTLY stripped of my freedom. March 20th, 2024. In no way, shape or form could I have been prepared or polished for this inevitable event. As excited as I was to be released from Bexar County, riding in that white SUV early in the morning, I would never be able to prepare for what was about to happen. Let's backtrack to summarize the way I landed on these grounds. January 12th, 2021. I took the Devil's Cup behind the wheel of my vehicle and the impatience and immaturity. Due to it, once again, relationship gone wrong, miscarriage and sadness, I ran a red light and wrecked that weapon into an innocent mother like myself. I caused Mrs. F. trauma, PTSD, and a minor hip fracture she never deserved. I pray she forgives me, and I will pray for her till my last breath. I was in denial if I ever thought alcohol didn't ruin things. It ruined my relationships, my health, my thoughts, my confidence. Physically it hurt Mrs.F and myself. My daughter has been a witness of this whole process which I pray she consumes as a learning experience live and in action. Being here in jail/ devilcation, I have not only dove knee deep into my Bible to gain the knowledge and the wisdom in Proverbs, but to understand a deep, far more empowering way of life. I am forgiven, I am loved, and I am a child of the utmost higher power. My God, that's the confidence I embody now as I write this final commencement. I have held myself accountable for my words and how to effectively communicate. Those who are wise, say little. Ladies, I thank you for the constructive criticism during this time. I know I struggled with this and it's a privilege to have learned this with you all. to the greens reds and blues, soul sister readers thank you for giving me grace. The most important thing I would say to you ladies is to focus on yourself and your own recovery but be vulnerable and trust the process.

Gods will

....

FIRST AND SECOND CORINTHIANS BROUGHT MY INTIMATE LOVE AFFAIR with God and the Holy Spirit to surface. Ladies, wow, scripture literally peeled back the layers of my soul, and perfectly lined up with God's will, and plan for my life. If you remember, I started with the book of Jon, setting the tone and baseline of my astounding belief in my father my God, my ABBA. Now on my final day at my final flock, God's love for me and his purpose for my life are revealed through, ever so gracefully Corinthians, and now Galatians. I'm born again in the Holy Spirit. I'm relinquished, renewed and worthy of God's miraculous love. The peace I have deep in my soul is unexplainably present. Ladies, please pick up that Bible and fall in love with your God. It's divine and it's now time. Don't wait till you've tried everything your way. You don't have to hit rock bottom, let God be your rock your solid foundation. Get adopted into the family of your ABBA your father God. The Holy Spirit will immensely amaze you. Our purpose is to fulfill God's plan and we can do this with courage and grace through reading the Bible. Waiting for discharge y'all my paperwork is complete my days that were numbered have come to an end and I'm patiently waiting on my departure. I just had the best conversation with one of the spirit sparrows that I mentioned at the beginning of this journey. Mrs. Clay was the first monitor to asked me if I was OK and to tell me that God's plans for me in here was for the good. As we were conversing, I thanked her and let her know how she positively impacted my life. Ladies again, it's those short mini miracles that make an impact. That minute conversation gave me courage and strength to endure the unknown here at this place, I resided. As I said, before I have fallen into an astounding miraculous intimate relationship with my Abba God, my father. Deeper than any words could ever describe. I wanted to thank her for being so kind, compassionate and believing In me and I did as we said our goodbyes. I asked for her first name, but oops that's illegal so I told her to look for my book, this book

"The flock that braved me."

Printed in the United States
by Baker & Taylor Publisher Services